ONE FOOT
ON THE GROUND

A Pilot's Memoirs of Aviators and Aviation

By Paul Roxin

ATC Press ▪ Rochester, NY ▪ 1998

Printed in the USA

Previous publication information:
ISBN.0-9663313-0-3 (softcover)
ISBN 0-9663313-1-1 (cloth)
LC No. TL540.R69 1998
Dewey Decimal No. 629.13'092   QBI98-249
LCCN Number: 98-84581
First Edition: July 1998
Book design by Mary Whitney Graphics
Second Edition: April 2003
Third Edition: December 2004

For further information contact:
ATC Press
84 Irving Road
Rochester, New York   14618
585-271-1960

Library of Congress Control Number 2004366680
National Library of Canada Cataloguing in Publication

Roxin, Paul
    ONE FOOT ON THE GROUND / Paul I. Roxin.
Includes bibliographical references and index.
ISBN 1-4120-0297-4
    I. Title.
TL539.R69 2003 629.13'092'274789 C2003-903084-9

111 Humboldt Street, Rochester, NY 14609
Phone   585.482.7770
Fax   585.482.7039
Web site www.rygan.com
E-mail   info@rygan.com
10   9   8   7   6   5   4   3   2

*For the 40,000 air men and women
of the 8th Air Force and their families —
so they will never be forgotten.*

Table of Contents

Acknowledgments

I always knew writing a book was a collaborative effort and want to thank the following people who have assisted in bringing this project to life. Excedrin also helped!

Special thanks to Mary Whitney for her beautiful design and layout of the book and to Frank Judge, Peter Heinrich and Stephen Goldstein for their invaluable and tireless editorial assistance and advice in shaping my thoughts.

Thanks to the editors and publishers of Gannett Rochester Newspapers — the *Democrat & Chronicle* and the sorely missed *Times-Union* — and the former Wolfe Newspapers, in which versions of several of the chapters previously appeared as articles.

To the following editors, writers, and critics who provided me with the inspiration and encouragement to undertake this project: Mark Hare, Douglas Sherman, Sharon Dickman, M. Kathleen Wagner, Virginia Smith, and Janet Lovejoy of Gannett; Linda Quinlan of the *Brighton-Pittsford Post*; Kathy Kelly of the Little Falls *Evening Times*; Bobbi Blood and Joseph Maher of the Schenectady *Daily Gazette*.

To Millie Courtemanche, who assisted in typing and proofreading many of the original articles; to Paul Ferguson, Clara Judge, and Jim Kraus, who did additional proofing and checking; to Laurie Klapp, Kristin Kieffer and Grace Ann Pierce of Kinko's East Rochester and to Cheryl R. Eckert of Gene Eckert Bookbinders for her excellent work producing the finished product.

And of course, to my family — my wife Beatrice, who endured every stage of this project with me; our daughter, Wendy Shinay, her husband, John, and their children, David and Brittany; our daughter, Deborah Waltzer, her husband, Donald, and their daughter, Lisa; and our son Richard, his wife, Kristine, and their daughters, Madison and Haley. Without their unfailing support and encouragement, this dream would not have been realized.

Credits

Cover photo courtesy of Joseph Kiseleski. Back cover photo of the author courtesy of Kevin Higley, Rochester *Democrat & Chronicle*. Correspondence between Eleanor Roosevelt and Amelia Earhart (Personal Letters, Series 100, 1933–Ea-Ga) courtesy of The Franklin Delano Roosevelt Library, Hyde Park, New York. Aerial photo of Curtiss Condor crash provided by Ruth Busacker, curator, Little Falls Historical Society Museum. Drawing of Curtiss-Wright T-32 Condor, *An American Siberia,* by Robert Parkes, reprinted from *Ernest K. Gann's Flying Circus*, Macmillan, 1974. Edward "Butch" O'Hare photo courtesy of the Chicago Airport System. Photo of the B-24 "Getaway Gertie" wing courtesy of H. Lee White Marine Museum, Oswego, New York. Geriatric Pilots Association logo by Carol Perkins. Photo of Rochester plane crash on p. 9 reprinted from *Life* magazine. Photo of Don Zimmer provided by David Kubissa of the Elmira *Star-Gazette*, wedding photo of John Paul Vann and Mary Jane Allen courtesy of the Vann estate.

Foreword

It speaks volumes for the breadth of his interests that Paul Roxin both founded the Brighton Symphony Orchestra and co-founded the Geriatric Pilots Association — two diverse organizations still very lively today.

This is a heart-and-soul man whose enthusiasms are both unquenchable and contagious, so that when he cares deeply about things, as he does about aviation and music, others get caught up, too.

A free clarinet and lessons in the fifth grade, given through one of George Eastman's school benevolences, sparked a love of music — one that led eventually to the production of several light operas in the early 1980s and an abiding interest in the Rochester Philharmonic Orchestra.

And it was free flight lessons, earned through weekend work at the airport when he was just 15, that turned Paul into a lifelong lover of flying.

Aviation is at the center of this collection of articles, many of them published in area newspapers through the years. In an age that doesn't have many heroes, Paul Roxin helps to fill the gap with his stories of valor and endurance among pilots and others in war and in peace.

Men and women who made their mark in aviation need to be remembered, the more so since many have local ties. Bringing these stories together in one place now makes this possible. Readers, who will find that Paul has an eye for the dramatic, will be grateful for his initiative.

Desmond Stone
Editorial Page Editor, Retired
Rochester *Democrat & Chronicle*
Rochester, New York
June 1998

Preface

This collection of stories is the culmination of a lifetime of unceasing interest in aviation. All of them are based on my own personal experiences with a variety of aircraft and an even greater number of people flying them, some famous, some not so famous, but all fascinating in their own ways.

The events and adventures that I have recalled from the past have become alive once more as I resurrected them for this volume. It wasn't until I had been absent from aviation for some 25 years that I began to commit these memories to paper, thanks in part to an invitation to attend a banquet of the Rochester Pilots Association (RPA) in 1980. My attendance at this banquet proved to be a fortuitous occasion, because I was given the opportunity to share my recollections with the group. Happily, I was invited to become a board member.

During this time, I became reacquainted with a number of veteran World War II aviators, contemporaries of mine, and we soon discovered that there were others who had shared similar experiences. After a piece by Carol Ritter appeared in a local newspaper about the formation of our group, a surprising number of former pilots showed up for subsequent meetings. I credit a flying buddy of mine, Cyril "Cy" Noon, for coining the name of our group, the Geriatric Pilots Association, a name that always seems to elicit a chuckle from those who hear about us.

Not surprisingly, nearly all of us had some sort of story to tell. For my part, I feel fortunate that I have had the opportunity to meet and know many of the people I have written about, and I am indebted to the other fliers who have shared their stories with me. Still many more stories remain to be told, and I hope that others will be forthcoming.

I can trace my own fascination with flying back to 1923, when at the tender age of seven, I was transfixed when a biplane swooped down to treetop level at No. 26 school in Rochester. By the age of 15, I was working as a "grease monkey" at the airport.

Back then, I also hawked plane rides to airport visitors — it was the only way I could get free flying lessons. It came as no surprise that some visitors had cold feet, telling us they'd be willing to go up as long as they could keep one foot on the ground. We had a pat response: "OK, we'll put a box of sand in the plane for you." It usually worked.

That stayed with me, and I named this collection of stories in tribute to those days.

My ultimate dream was realized in 1936, when I got my pilot's license. During the war years of the '40s, I served as a ground-school instructor for the Air Force. Fortunately, many recollections of those days have remained vividly etched in my mind, and I hope this collection will serve as a legacy our descendants can look back upon fondly.

This work isn't intended to be comprehensive. Much of it consists of anecdotes, names and places recognizable primarily to upstate New York pilots and residents who recall World War II. But I trust the events I have recounted will have a universal interest.

The Geriatric Pilots Association currently numbers more than 160 former pilots, including a cadre of speakers who speak at high schools and before other interested groups. In a number of instances, the GPA has taken a resolute stand against those revisionists who have distorted and selectively chosen facts in an attempt to rewrite history to fit their own agenda.

For those who are not members of the GPA, I encourage you to contact us. The GPA can be reached at 84 Irving Road, Rochester, New York 14618

We'd love to swap old stories with you!

Paul I. Roxin
July 1998

Paul Roxin, 18 years old, building up hours to get his private license.

Dwight Turner and John Ransier in Hollandia, New Guinea, 1944.

Oops! Look what happens when the engine decides to quit and you land on a muddy field. Pilot Fred McGinn was unhurt.

Gerald Wilmot, Bill Odom and Mayor Sam Dicker in front of Beechcraft Bonanza.

United Boeing 247 landed in Rochester in August, 1933 to avoid severe thunderstorms.

Rochester Aviation

Rochester's Skilled Pilots

Cyril Noon with his wife, Zona, in 1943.

More than a few Rochesterians who flew during World War II experienced some noteworthy incidents. One of them dates back to 1944, when Capt. Cyril "Cy" Noon prevailed upon his superiors to allow his wife, Zona, to accompany him on a flight of a B-17 Flying Fortress.

Cy, who was a test pilot in the Air Force, borrowed a parachute for Zona, who occupied the co-pilot's seat while a neophyte co-pilot was given another assignment.

The Flying Fortress, which also had a crew chief on board, had just undergone a two-hour inspection and was now groomed for the test flight.

Preparing for takeoff, Cy set the manifold pressure for all four engines at 49 pounds per square inch (psi), gently pushed all four throttles forward, and barreled down the runway.

Reaching 85 mph, he gently eased back on the control column and lifted the bomber off the runway. No sooner was he airborne than the manifold pressure in No. 1 engine shot up to 89 psi.

Cy instantly pulled back the throttle, but it was too late, and the engine burst into flames with the plane barely 50 feet in the air. He called a "mayday" to the control tower, gained a bit more altitude, stuck the plane up on a wing, swung around, and prepared for an emergency landing.

At this point, Zona and the crew chief could see flames and black smoke pouring from the nacelle of the burning engine. Cy safely landed the B-17, and the entire crew quickly evacuated the plane while emergency crews poured foam on the burning engine.

The mishap was caused by a mechanic's failure to insert a cotter pin locking a nut on a bolt of the engine's supercharger. The bolt fell out, and all hell broke loose.

With a burning engine, not many pilots would be able to keep their cool, but Cy Noon did. Thanks to his quick thinking, the crew survived and a B-17 was saved to fight the war.

It was July of 1945, Marty Nacman, now a Brighton resident, was a crew member of a squadron of C-47s returning to the Trinidad AFB in the States to be outfitted and transferred to the Pacific.

When one of the C-47s was about 100 miles out, it ran into a severe thunderstorm. Because of the turbulence, the plane bounced like a cork on water, and then the starboard engine conked out.

In an effort to keep airborne, the pilot feathered the engine and ordered the crew to jettison all cargo. When the plane broke out of the storm, barely maintaining altitude, the pilot tried his radio but found it dead. He asked the co-pilot to try his, but it also was dead.

"Have the crew chief check the fuses," he ordered. A few moments later, the co-pilot returned and reported, "You won't believe this. You know that our transmitters have handles so if a radio malfunctions, a mechanic at any base can remove the drawer and insert a new transmitter. Well, when you ordered the jettison of all cargo, guess what one crew member did to the radio equipment?! He tossed it into the Atlantic!" (The plane landed safely at Trinidad Airport, evoking the quip "any landing you can walk away from is a good landing.")

If there ever was a local edition of the *Guinness Book of World Records* with a category for which a Rochesterian commuted the greatest distance to get to work, one contender would be Captain Fred McGinn of Pittsford. McGinn was based at Kennedy Airport in New York, about 310 miles from Rochester. He would board a morning flight here and that afternoon would pick up his normal JFK-San Francisco run in a DC-10, returning to Kennedy and Rochester the following day.

McGinn was a pilot with American Airlines before he retired several years ago.

Tailspin Tommy

When the Rochester *Times-Union* ceased operations Friday, June 27, 1997, a source of knowledge, inspiration, and entertainment came to a sad ending.

From the stage of learning to read, I was enamored with the comic strips "Mutt & Jeff" and "Ella Cinders." But the newspaper cartoon most influential in setting the course for my career chronicled the daily exploits of "Tailspin Tommy," who began his career as a "grease monkey" (nowadays a "line boy") at a small airport. His duties consisted of cleaning airplanes and selling rides in what I recall was a World War I "Jenny," a three-seat biplane.

In due time, he learned to fly, became a commercial pilot, and then flew the U.S. Mail, which to me epitomized the ultimate career in life, something very impressive to an 11-year-old.

With Charles Lindbergh's flight from New York to Paris in May 1927, aviation became more commonplace as many airlines began operations in this country. None of this would have been possible had it not been for the concern of Harry Guggenheim, who provided the financing for the development of many of the "blind" instruments, airways, and controlled-pitch propellers, among others.

During this period, a syndicated cartoonist depicted a forthcoming problem for aviation — traffic control. Ahead of his time, the artist displayed a policeman, akin to a Keystone cop, in the basket of a balloon, a whistle in his mouth and a billy club in his right hand, barking orders like a traffic cop to planes whizzing by the balloon... a farfetched concept of control but recognizing a future problem with the embryonic industry.

In the early '30s, some of the major airports, such as Newark, Cleveland, and Chicago, created their own control towers, mostly by using a hand-held light with green, red, and white reflectors — with the appropriate colors beamed at the airplane. In some areas, radio communication between the towers and the planes became a reality when the frequency of 278 khz was designated for tower use.

It wasn't until the summer of 1935 that the Rochester Airport inaugurated the first control tower, an affirmation of the adage "Necessity is the mother of invention."

Flying buddies Paul Roxin, Baron Brodine and Elmer Page, 1934.

It all happened one beautiful Sunday evening, when Clarence Robinson, along with his younger brother, Kent, operating as Robinson Air Service, was returning from a charter flight from Buffalo, and made a straight-in approach on the Northeast runway. At the same time, Elmer Page (who worked for Ray Hylan) landed on the south runway with two passengers.

The two planes were a brand new $15,000 Stinson Reliant flown by Clarence and a $900 Waco biplane flown by Elmer. Both planes met at the intersection of the runways, neither pilot having seen the other. Boom! The propeller of the Waco chewed about two feet off the Reliant's wing.

The following day, "Robby" sued Hylan, the owner of the Waco, and Ray immediately countersued. However, in those days, a good deal of common sense prevailed, and the attorneys for both sides convinced their clients that neither was at fault. The problem was "no control tower."

Howard Shafer, the airport manager, immediately made plans for installing a tower, which was constructed in 10 days, once the control lights arrived, and some rules and regulations were put in place.

The tower was located on the northeast corner of hanger #2, directly above the airport operations office, where the U.S. Weather Bureau offices later were located. There was a problem with the many dead spots — about 60 percent of the viewing area was obstructed by the brick structure, but it was better than nothing at all.

One afternoon in the late spring of 1936, another accident occurred. This time, Dr. James Watson, flying his Fairchild 24, approached on the Southwest runway, and Elmer Page, once again flying a Waco F, approached on the Northwest runway. Elmer's plane was in the blind spot of the tower operator, Carl Reiniger, who had given a green light to "Doc" Watson.

The two planes collided about 15 feet off the ground where the two runways crossed, forming a large letter "X". The Fairchild dug its nose into the ground, but Watson wasn't injured and Elmer again escaped without any damage to himself. The Waco sustained slight damage, and the Fairchild wound up on its nose, with considerable damage. Raw gasoline was flowing from the ruptured carburetor, and Doc just lit a cigarette to calm his nerves. I vividly recall Guy Stratton, my boss, calling this to his attention and the congenial Doc snuffed out his cigarette.

There was no question that if not for the blind spots in the tower, the accident could have been averted. The solution was a new tower

The "new" tower at the Monroe County Airport. Photo by Bernie Newmark.

free of blind spots. Howard Shafer again went to work. A new 40-foot steel tower with gondola-type cab was erected as a temporary stop gap about 100 feet from the operations office on Scottsville Road. There was a mostly clear view of the entire area except to the south. Plans called for building a permanent tower as soon as possible.

But in spite of the best intentions, the complications of World War II interrupted those plans for some 13 years. In 1949, the Civil Aeronautics Administration assumed control of traffic at the airport, and put in its own personnel. With George Freitag as tower chief, the CAA built a new state-of-the-art structure complete with two-way radio and, most importantly, a clear view of the entire field.

Propeller Tips and Bits

An unorthodox landing.

The following scene is based upon an incident that happened in the early 1930s at the Rochester Airport. Setting the stage are a grandfather and his 12-year-old grandson, Billy.

Billy: "Grandpa, what did you used to do for a living?"

Grandfather: "Well, among other things, I used to operate a steam-roller at the Rochester Airport."

Billy: "What's a steamroller, Gramps?"

Grandfather: "Well, it was something like a locomotive. It was invented shortly after the Civil War and was primarily used for building roads. At the airport, it was used to smooth out the runways. You see, in the early days of aviation, runways weren't made of concrete but cinders."

Billy: "But why did you have to smooth them out?"

Grandfather: "Because most of the aircraft were biplanes, and instead of a tail wheel they had a skid. Every time a plane landed, took off, or taxied, it left a three-inch groove, which made the runway extremely rough. So about twice a week, it was my job to roll the runways."

Billy: "Gee, that doesn't sound very exciting."

Grandfather: "Well, let me tell you about something that happened one day that even the Three Stooges couldn't dream up."

Billy: "What was that, Grandpa?"

Grandfather: "Well, the nose of this plane was higher than the cockpit, creating a blind spot directly ahead. So when the pilot taxied the plane, he had to bob his head from one side to the other to make sure there were no obstructions or other aircraft in his path.

"On this particular day, having just finished my assignment, I was returning the steamroller to its storage area when a student pilot carelessly began taxiing straight for the steamroller.

"I naturally tried to maneuver out of the way, but he was moving too fast to avoid a collision. Just before he struck, I jumped off and ran off in the opposite direction as fast as my legs would carry me. And then BOOM! The nose of the plane hit the steamroller, smashing the wooden Hartzell propeller to smithereens (the steamroller suffered no visible damage). This meant the plane was grounded for a few days until we got a replacement prop.

"I suppose the *Guinness Book of World Records* should authenticate the event as the first known collision between an airplane and a steamroller. And it happened right here on Scottsville Road!"

Speaking of propellers, in the winter of 1936, a pilot named George Koenlein rented Clarence Robinson's Kinner Fleet for a short hop over the northeastern section of Rochester. Whilethe plane was over the city, the propeller flew off the engine, forcing George to look for a place to set the plane down. He made a valiant effort to land at the Avenue D playground between Conkey Avenue and Hollenbeck Street, but the craft fell short by about 30 feet, crashing into a tree at the rear of 43 Bleile Terrace, two houses from the playground.

It was a most remarkable landing. With the plane perched in the treetop, the pilot climbed out of the cockpit unscathed.

A group from the airport arrived at the scene and had quite a job removing the plane, but apart from holes caused by tree branches, the plane was pretty much intact. It was completely checked over and was airborne again in about two weeks. And because the emergency landing was unique, a picture of the plane appeared in *Life* magazine a few weeks later.

And what became of the propeller? It came down on Sullivan Street, halfway between Joseph Avenue and Clinton Avenue North.

A few years later, Ralph Burford, who worked for Pete Barton, owner of Rochester Aeronautical Corp., invited George Cheatham to fly Pete's Fairchild 24. After about a 10-minute hop, the plane landed but sat there on the runway. In the meantime, I had taxied out with a student named Andrew Townsend and pulled alongside Ralph and George, who had made no effort to leave the runway.

There was something strange about their plane. At first, I was puzzled, but when the doors on both sides of the cabin opened simultaneously, and Ralph and George started to push the plane off the runway, I shouted, "Holy smoke! No propeller!"

The entire crankshaft and propeller were missing, and what George had done was a "dead-stick landing," which in the vernacular means engine failure. Fortunately, he was able to glide to a safe landing at the airport.

Later that day, George was teased by some of his fellow pilots: "What happened, George? Did the rubber band on your model airplane break?"

In 1938, George went to work for Braniff Airlines and eventually became its chief pilot. Ralph flew for American Airlines as a captain for many years.

Recently, the media carried an account of the flight of Douglas "Wrong Way" Corrigan, who in 1938 supposedly departed from New York for California and instead wound up several hours later in Ireland, the home of his ancestors.

Upon his return from this history-making flight, he toured the States and received a hero's welcome wherever he visited. However, in Rochester, he landed his rickety old J6-5 Curtiss Robin, and an embarrassing incident occurred.

When Doug pulled up to the underground gas pit between hangers 1 and 2, Tommy Greenwood, an airport employee, opened the door to greet the hero, and the entire door came off in Tommy's hands. One of the mechanics soon repaired the broken hinges, and Corrigan moved on to his next stop.

Incidentally, Doug was with the Air Transport Command during World War II, ferrying planes all over the world, and word had it that he never got lost!

A final story about propellers: During World War II, an aviation cadet was practicing landings in an AT-6, which had a retractable landing gear. On his last approach, the tower operator noticed the plane coming in with its wheels still up. The tower advised him: "Air Force 9125, either take it around again or lower your landing gear." When the pilot failed to respond, the controller anxiously repeated the command several times — to no avail.

The plane landed on its belly, and the propeller bit into the concrete and was bent into the shape of a pretzel. Sparks flew everywhere as the plane ground-looped off the runway and onto its nose, its tail pointing skyward. Fortunately, the cadet wasn't injured.

A few days later, a board of inquiry met to investigate the cause of the accident. Following the testimony of the airport traffic controller, the officer conducting the meeting asked the cadet, "Didn't you hear the instructions to take it around again or lower the landing gear?"

"No, sir!" the young cadet replied in all sincerity. "That horn was making so much noise, I couldn't hear a word he was saying."

The horn was the warning signal to alert the pilot that the landing gear was still up.

Early Pilot Shenanigans

This tale, concerning two local pilots, could be construed as a take-off on Eugene O'Neill's *The Iceman Cometh*, except this tale should be named "The Iceman Slippeth."

Johnny Wiley delivered ice for a living and first showed up at the Rochester Airport during the winter of 1933. He always flew an old Waco 10 with a World War I OX-5 engine owned by a resident of Gorham, New York.

Johnny would break every rule in the book on safety. He'd make steep, climbing turns or 90-degree vertical banks on takeoff. If the engine had so much as sneezed, there would be only one direction his plane could go — down. Somehow, despite all his hair-raising stunts, he and his passenger survived all the shenanigans.

One day, Johnny, who had rented Ray Hylan's black and red Waco F, slipped a bit too close to the ground. He sheared off the landing gear, bent the propeller, and sustained other damages to the wing estimated at about $600 — in those days you could buy an entire used Waco for about $1,200!

To defray the repair costs, Ray and Johnny decided to raffle off a new car, with the profits going to Hylan for the repairs. Tickets were about 25 cents, and literally thousands of them were sold around town.

But nothing stated where or when the raffle would be held. So, we came to work one morning to learn the drawing had been held in Hylan's office the previous evening. Nobody from the field was present, and the lucky winner was none other than Ray Hylan himself. That was the last raffle ever held at the Rochester Airport!

During the last few years of his life, whenever I'd visit Ray, he always wanted to discuss "the good old days," but somehow we never managed to recall this particular little stunt.

Ray Hylan
Rochester's Aviation Icon
1933

Intestinal fortitude at its best!

Ray's "Pride and Joy," a Boeing F4B-4, a gift to the Smithsonian Institution in 1959.

Much to everyone's surprise, Charles Lindbergh (second from right) showed up at the Rochester Airport one fine day. He's pictured here with, from left, Roy Alexander and pilots Love, Brandeweide and Dahlman.

Tales of Early Planes and Fliers

Occasionally I wonder how many of us have gone through life telling a favorite story but, after countless repetitions, eventually we ask ourselves: "Did this really happen, or is it a figment of my imagination?"

This is a tale that might fall into that category.

During the summer of 1936, a group of about 10 fellow fliers sat around the airport manager's office hoping a few passengers might show up willing to spend $1.50 apiece for a ride.

About 3 pm one July afternoon, a Monocoupe, which was a high-wing monoplane normally powered by a 90-horsepower Lambert engine, circled the Rochester Airport. We all immediately knew by the sound of the engine that it was a Warner Scarab, 125 horsepower. That plane had wheel pants, and each wing had about one foot clipped off. With those modifications, the plane could add an extra 15 mph of cruising speed.

Because the sun was beating down on our cinder runways, creating some thermal and turbulent conditions, it was common for a plane to bounce slightly upon landing, which happened with the itinerant Monocoupe.

At this point, being all of 19 years old with a brand-new private license, I nudged Elmer "Skinny" Page and commented, "When that pilot taxies in, send him over, and I'll give him a few pointers on how to land an airplane."

A few moments later, the pilot was guided to an in-ground gas pit located between hangars No. 1 and 2. My boss, Guy Stratton, picked himself up and walked around the parked aircraft to admire its smooth lines.

When he gazed into the cockpit, his jaw dropped about a foot.

The pilot of that Monocoupe — the one I had told Elmer to send over to me for a few tips on landing a plane, was none other than Charles Lindbergh, accompanied by his wife, Anne.

Climbing out of the cockpit, Lindbergh made two requests.

First he said, "Please don't notify the newspapers."

Then he added, "Please don't take any pictures, and we'll both be happy to answer any questions."

Needless to say, for 15 minutes or so, the 10 of us enjoyed the company of the Lindberghs.

After the plane had refueled, the couple left for Cleveland.

For more than 50 years I've retold this story, and with the passing of time, self-doubts had started gnawing at my memory.

Had it actually happened?

A few years ago, while attending a Rochester Pilots Association event, I was talking with my old friend Art Lohman, and I asked him, "Do you recall the incident back in 1936 when Lindbergh landed in Rochester?"

His reply was spontaneous and affirmative. "I sure do! He was flying a souped-up Monocoupe powered by a Warner engine, a sleek-looking plane."

I replied, "Thanks, Art. For a while, I thought I was losing my marbles."

Another incident a year earlier — 1935 — jogs my memory. It was a beautiful spring day, and an American Airlines Stinson Tri-Motor departing from Rochester had just cleared the high-tension wires about a half-mile southwest of the airport. Suddenly, all engines quit, and the pilot successfully put the plane down in a field with hardly a scratch.

At that time, Rochester had two afternoon papers, the *Times-Union* and the *Journal-American*. Each week, the *Journal* would award a $20 prize for the best story phoned in.

Of course, as soon as word spread about the American Airlines plane, everyone on the field, including me, called the *Journal*.

A few days later, Jim Wilmot, who at the time was the assistant airport manager, called me aside and said: "You were about the sixth one to report the story, and I happened to be the first. But if I'm awarded the prize, I could be fired from my $30-a-week job. So why don't I arrange for you to get the prize, and we'll split the 20 bucks?"

"It's a deal," I happily replied, and a few days later we split the award.

Incidentally, what apparently happened was that the plane had fueled in Syracuse and took on additional gas at Rochester. Apparently, there was water in the tank at Syracuse, because three planes gassed up from the same pit in Rochester — an Army observation plane, a Bellanca flown by a Dr. Light from Strong Memorial Hospital, and, of course, the Stinson. Neither of the other two planes loading up here with fuel had any problem.

Shortly after the accident, a crew of mechanics arrived from Buffalo, dismantled the plane, and towed the fuselage to hangar No. 2, where the wings were reassembled, and the next day, the plane was flown to Buffalo for a complete overhaul.

As a postscript, in the early days, American Airlines Inc. was known as American Airways Inc. and flew mail. Among the pilots flying the hazardous job were Cy Bittner, Ernie Bashin, and Ernie Dryer. During the terrible Depression, the pilots would receive 5 cents per mile for daylight operations and 10 cents per mile for nighttime.

The airlines used to get $5 per pound per airline mile, hardly enough to meet expenses, so occasionally a 5-pound ordinary brick would somehow wind up in the mail sack.

Whereas "neither rain, nor hail, nor sleet shall keep them from their appointed rounds" and so forth, there was a Depression on, and Chapter 11 bankruptcy protection wasn't even a dream for anybody. Therefore, steps like that were occasionally taken to keep the airline from becoming a "fly by night" operation.

"Winnie" Churchill, Rochester Pilot

History buffs may wish to test and amuse themselves with this true and false exercise:

1. Winston Churchill's mother was born in Brooklyn, New York.

    True   False

2. Part of her early childhood was spent in Palmyra, New York.

    True   False

3. For a time, Winston Churchill was a used car dealer with showrooms on Mt. Hope Avenue.

    True   False

4. Winston Churchill owned and flew his own airplane.

    True   False

If you answered "true" for all of the questions, you got a perfect score.

But, some explanation is probably in order for most of you.

Items 1 and 2 applied to "Winnie" Churchill, the renowned prime minister of England, who successfully guided the British Empire to victory during World War II.

But items 3 and 4, concerned Rochester's own "Winnie" Churchill, who actually owned a used car agency on Mt. Hope Avenue from the early '30s through the '60s. Winnie was basically a weekend flyer who owned a four-place Ryan Monoplane.

In the early '30s, he took a cross-country jaunt to Texas and then decided to continue on into Mexico. Because weather reporting facilities in Mexico were almost nonexistent, he telephoned his destination for the latest weather, field conditions, and so forth. In response to his name and type of plane, he replied, "Winston Churchill, the plane Ryan, the same company which built the *Spirit of St. Louis.*"

When our local resident landed at his destination, he was greeted by the mayor, a hastily erected reviewing stand, a brass band, and hundreds of local residents. When the mayor asked, "Where is Mr. Churchill?" Winnie calmly replied, "*I'm* Mr. Churchill."

"But we were expecting the great statesman from England," the mayor exclaimed.

"Sorry to disappoint you," he replied, "but I'm no statesman — just a used car salesman from Rochester, New York."

A 1933 photo. From rear left: unknown, Edgar DeLano, Walt Young, Clarence Robinson, Seyle Whitmore, Joe Mirguet, Harold Brown, Howard Shafer, Spencer Punnet, Ralph Barton, Vic Evans, unknown, Ray Hylan, Guy Stratton, George Cheatham, Winston Churchill, Bill Earith, Walt Gosnell, unknown, and Chuck McNabb. Front row: Russ Holderman, Al Williams, Dick Richards, Jack Jenkins, Elmer Page, Claude Herrick, and Barron Brodine.

A Flying Circus:
Early Years of Flight Had Plenty of Character

In 1924, when Simon "Cy" Bittner decided to forsake the coal mines of southwestern Pennsylvania and join the famed Gates Flying Circus both as a parachute jumper and wing-walker, he never dreamed his flight instructor, Charles Lindbergh, would become an international hero by making a solo flight from New York to Paris three years later.

Better known as "Shorty" and every bit of 5 feet, 4 inches tall, Cy could conjure up more unbelievable pranks, leading aviation buffs to refer to him as the *Till Eulenspeigel* (Merry Prankster) of the airways.

During the late 1920s, while serving as a flight instructor at Albany, Shorty had a student named Clyde Saylor, who had the skill to solo but lacked the confidence. So, Cy decided to cure his reluctant student of his phobia.

Prior to Clyde's arrival, Shorty, who had been a parachute jumper with the Gates Flying Circus, stuck his parachute into the front cockpit of the OX-5 Waco 10. After take-off, he told Clyde to climb to 2,000 feet.

When they reached 2,000 feet, Shorty harnessed up his chute, unscrewed the control stick, unbuckled his safety belt and jumped out of the plane, leaving a petrified Clyde up there alone! Eventually Clyde landed safely, but it was a long time before he appeared at the airport again.

One of Shorty's many transgressions as an airmail pilot for Colonial Airways (which later became American) occurred one beautiful moonlit night, when he spotted a New York Central train speeding through the Montezuma Swamp near Clyde, New York. With his navigation lights turned off, he descended to about 20 feet, headed straight at the train, and, when he was about 1,000 feet from the approaching train, he turned on one landing light. This gave the startled engineer the horrifying impression that another train was barreling down the track on a head-on collision course.

At the last moment, Shorty pulled up and continued on his flight. Rumor has it you could see sparks flying for miles around when the engineer slammed on his brakes. He must have flattened every wheel on the train. But apart from the fact that passengers were thrown from their seats and baggage was flung about, the train resumed its journey. The flabbergasted engineer couldn't imagine where the phantom locomotive had come from or disappeared to — until a few days later, when Shorty confessed to being the culprit and apologized. All was forgiven.

In 1929, when I was in the 8th grade at the old Washington Junior High, I earned money as a newsboy selling the *Times-Union* and *Journal-American* across from the Eastman Theater. I was yelling "Extra! Extra! Read all about It! Prisoners riot at Auburn State Prison!"

A few years later, while working part time at the airport, I learned the facts of Shorty's involvement in the rebellion. When refueling in Syracuse en route to Rochester, Shorty learned of the riot and decided to get a bird's eye view of what was happening. So, down went the nose of his Pitcairn, below the walls and onto the prison yard. The prison guards, fearing this might be part of the riot, began shooting at the plane, but Shorty escaped unscathed. This was probably the first actual aerial observation of an uprising at a prison.

A few days later, Shorty had an appointment with a New York banker, hoping to obtain the necessary backing for a solo flight across the Atlantic. He was ushered into the would-be sponsor's plush office,

Simon "Shorty" Bittner

but before he could sit down, the banker thrust a newspaper into his face and asked: "Are you the same person?" Shorty took one look at the glaring headlines, which read, "Airmail pilot participates in prison riot" and made a hasty retreat for the nearest exit.

My first encounter with Shorty occurred one afternoon in late March of 1936. Because of a heavy fog, the American flight was cancelled here. Shorty, and my boss, Guy Stratton, who flew the mail with Shorty a few years back, were sitting in our office when Cy spotted my saxophone in a corner.

"Can you play a tune on it?" he asked.

"Just one. A piece called 'Stars Fell on Alabama,' " I said. At which Shorty invited us into the cockpit of his parked plane and turned on the radio equipment, and I proceeded to make aviation history. The number was broadcast over the entire American Airlines radio system, and Shorty remarked that I wailed "like Mrs. O'Leary's cow got her tail caught in the barn door." He gave me $1 to make myself and my saxophone scarce, but with that buck, I was able to run the Model A Ford I had purchased from Jim Wilmot for the entire week.

One night, with Rochester's own Vic Evans as co-pilot, Shorty landed at the airport. There were no passengers on the plane, and when the cabin door was opened, there were newspapers, magazines and cushions strewn all over the interior.

When I asked Vic what happened, he replied: "We were flying over Batavia at 3,000 feet, when Shorty asked me: 'I wonder how this loops?' 'How should I know? I never looped a Tri-Motor,' I told him.

"Shorty said: 'Let's find out.' So down went the nose of the Stinson airplane and, after reaching 150 mph, he pulled back on the wheel, and completed a perfect loop, just as he had done hundreds of times. And that's when everything was thrown around the cabin."

When *Gone With The Wind* was to have its world premiere in Atlanta in 1939, MGM chartered an American DC-3 to carry Clark Cable, Carole Lombard, and a host of other Hollywood dignitaries to the gala event. Guess who was selected as the captain of the flight? Right, Shorty!

And Clark Gable was so taken with Shorty's sense of humor and skill that he invited him to be his personal guest at the premiere. Regretfully, Cy had to decline because American Airlines had a policy forbidding flight personnel from appearing in public in uniform. And guess who didn't have a change of clothes?

After Pearl Harbor, Shorty divorced his first wife and married a stewardess. He eventually divorced her and planned to remarry his first wife and travel to Alaska for a second honeymoon. But fate intervened when Shorty, by then retired, suffered a massive stroke. He died in a nursing home in Cleveland in 1984.

At his funeral, in what was referred to as the "urology," the farewell remarks were devoted to many of Shorty's escapades, including the incident when, with a new stewardess aboard, he set the plane on automatic pilot, rang for her to come to the cockpit, and he and the co-pilot hid in a forward baggage compartment. When the poor girl found the cockpit empty, she turned white and let out a shriek that was heard all the way to the rear of the DC-3.

Upon the defeat of Germany in May 1945, President Truman ordered Gen. Eisenhower to return to the States for a grand victory celebration. Who was his pilot? None other than Shorty, the former coal miner-turned aviator, a prankster who never lost his sense of humor. Nor in his entire career did he ever as much put a scratch on an airplane. He was one pilot who always managed to keep *both* feet on the ground.

*American Airlines
Capt. Al Austin,
formerly of
Bloomfield, NY,
at Elmira Airport,
1953.*

*Guy Stratton,
my boss, 1934*

*Paul Roxin "props" a
Monocoupe at the Monroe
County Airport. Rochester
made Cunningham-Hall
(still flying) in background.*

*Arnold Eckert in the front
seat of a Piper J3.*

*Gannett Newspaper Stinson Reliant,
about 1948.*

World War II

Eugene M. Beattie, originally from Rochester, New York, was an American Airlines pilot for a number of years. He flew the North Atlantic during World War II ferrying aircraft to and from the European Theatre of operations, as part of the Air Transport Command. After the war he returned to American Airlines, and then became chief pilot for the General Electric Company.

In 1963, Gene passed away, which was a great loss to the aviation industry, and he was a perfect example of a truly exemplary citizen. It was the Gene Beatties of this era whom Tom Brokaw dubbed the "The Greatest Generation."

Rochester During World War II

Lt. Gordon Root (left) of Victor was killed in 1944 in a P51 accident. Capt. Fred McGinn became a pilot for American Airlines in 1943 and flew for them for 34 years.

Fliers Knew the Area Well

At the outbreak of World War II, Rochester ranked about 22nd in the nation in population. But when it came to producing pilots to man various aircraft — whether civilian, military, or commercial — the city outstripped many larger communities in the country.

In his book, *Fate is the Hunter*, Ernest Gann (co-pilot to Rochester's own Gene Beattie of American Airlines) mentioned the heavy traffic the pilots encountered approaching Rochester Airport in the late 1930s and early '40s. The reason for this congestion was that we had four very aggressive and successful flying schools operating at the airport, regularly churning out dozens of pilots — Page Airways, Hylan, Rochester Aeronautical Corp., and Rochester Flying School.

Gerald "Tiny" Wilmot, manager of Page Airways who doubled as a flight instructor (and who, like me, hated doing spins), recalled that "in early 1940, Washington got the brilliant idea to take advantage of the thousands of private planes and pilots — something other countries didn't possess — to encourage the growth of aviation. Our air force could be expanded at a rapid pace."

So, with England's back to the wall, the government sponsored the Civilian Pilot Training Program (CPT). The program awarded scholarships to promising candidates who completed a rigid ground-school program.

With the cooperation of the University of Rochester, selected students were given ground school courses and 40 hours of flight experience; upon passing the Civil Aeronautics Administration examination, they were awarded a private pilot's license.

The secondary program consisted of acrobatics using Waco UPF-7s, followed by the third stage of cross-country experience. With

successful completion of both, students would receive a commercial license, meaning they could obtain positions with the scheduled airlines or become flight instructors. With this undertaking, hundreds of pilots were locally trained. Following the attack on Pearl Harbor, many joined the services, usually receiving a commission.

But in September of 1942, Rochester Business Institute, under the direction

Capt. Clifford B. Schoenheit was commissioned as a Navigator during WWII, and later, matriculated again as a Cadet, and was commissioned as a pilot. This photo was taken in 1949.

of its active president, Ernest Veigel, secured a large CPT program, complete with uniforms left over from the Civilian Conservation Corps of the 1930s.

The purpose of the program was to train cadets as flight officers, to serve on troop-carrying gliders, or to fly the "Hump" in the China-Burma Theater.

Though the purpose of the quasi-official project was sound, its execution left much to be desired, and it was abandoned by Christmas of that year.

But by January 1943, RBI teamed with Hylan, Page, Rochester Aeronautical, and Holderman Flying Service and secured a large Army

-Air Corps contract that trained thousands of enlisted men (future officer material) to be pilots.

About 7,000 cadets arrived here from the classification center in Atlantic City, spent three months in Rochester, and then continued to Nashville for assignment as a pilot, navigator or bombardier.

As in communities across the nation, Rochesterians rallied in an all-out effort to win the war and opened their hearts to the cadets.

The War Changes Pilot Activities

When the news flashed on December 7, 1941, that a fleet of Japanese bombers had attacked Pearl Harbor, the initial reaction in Rochester was disbelief.

Many pilots at the field curtailed their operations and returned home to spend time with their families and to stay glued to the radio for whatever news might be forthcoming.

By midnight, every civilian aircraft was grounded, every pilot's license was suspended, and the only planes moving were the 200 flown by TWA, United, American, and other airlines, plus a sprinkling of military craft.

For the next three or four weeks, the only civilian aircraft operating in Rochester was a Stinson Reliant flown by Russ Holderman, whose job was to check compliance with blackout procedures — all street lights and neon signs were turned off, houses had to have their drapes drawn, and cars couldn't use headlights (in effect meaning they couldn't be driven). It was a frightening time, and it was Russ' job to report any deviations from these procedures.

In January 1942, the CPT Program was reactivated, and all pilots had to be recertified. All corporate aircraft were commandeered by Uncle Sam; even Gannett Newspapers' Lockheed 12 fell into that category.

With the passing of each week, the number of familiar faces at the airport diminished because many pilots were grabbed by the airlines or were offered commissions by the U.S. Air Corps, Navy, or Marine Corps.

Marshall Zinter, second from the left in the first rank of four and a Rochester native, was one of the first group of soldiers assigned to the C.T.D. in Rochester.

Rochester Contributed

The old Colgate Divinity School at East Avenue and Alexander Street served as barracks for cadets. Each morning, the entire contingent — 500 strong — banners flying, marched in tight formation chanting songs all the way from their dormitory on East Avenue to RBI, located across from Washington Square Park on Clinton Avenue South.

At the sounding of "Taps" at the end of the day, the colors were lowered and scores of Rochesterians, tears streaming down their cheeks, would silently observe. Everybody had a brother, a father, an uncle, a sister or a grandfather fighting this war of survival, but morale was very high.

Casualties were running high, and few families were spared the worry and, in many cases, the grief connected with this devastating conflict. This also was a period of tremendous solidarity among Americans, who were willing to do anything necessary to win the war as quickly as possible.

Among the CPT instructors was future Wilmorite board chairman, William "Wee" Wilmot. Wee was a natural pilot and, along with Fred McGinn, became a test pilot for Douglas Aircraft, a company that built thousands of C-47s at Tinker Field in Oklahoma.

He went on to the Air Ferry Command, ferrying just about every plane the Air Force had to the most remote parts of the world. This assignment included delivering the P-63 King Cobra to the Russians via Alaska and Siberia. Fred was hired by American Airlines and spent the next several years flying almost every model of plane American acquired.

Aircraft Parts Manufacturing

Although no airplanes were manufactured in Rochester, many firms contracted with the major aircraft builders to build various aircraft components. One such firm on University Avenue built parts of the landing gear for the Grumman Navy fighters. On one occasion, former Page Airways instructor, Dan Cohen — then a lieutenant with the Navy — flew an F4U Corsair to Rochester, folded up its wings, and had it towed to University Avenue so the workers could examine the fruits of their labor.

Incidentally, during an operation in the Pacific, a young Navy pilot once took off from an aircraft carrier in a fighter with its wings still folded. Though he actually got aloft, he was in danger of plummeting like a stone. But he miraculously managed to lower his wings and begin normal flight!

The Red Cross

The local chapter of the Red Cross played a dynamic role in providing indispensable air service during the war.

Rochester was the destination for many Navy hospital aircraft, which normally were R4Ds. The aircraft ferried injured and sick servicemen from the Pacific Theater to Samson Naval Base on Seneca Lake.

The local CAA office would immediately notify the local Red Cross upon receipt of a flight plan.

Regardless of the time of day or night, the Red Cross would greet the flight crews and patients, attending to the needs of the sick and injured before they were transferred to waiting ambulances.

Local Aviators Gave Their Lives

Among the local aviators who made the ultimate sacrifice for our country were Lt. Bill LePine, who was lost on a flight to Ascension Island; Lt. Gordon Root of Victor, whose P-51 crashed in Genesee Valley Park; and Sanford Schubiner, a civilian test pilot for Curtiss-Wright in Louisville, Kentucky, whose experimental plywood cargo plane disintegrated in flight.

One of the most bizarre incidents involving a pilot who settled in this area occurred in England just prior to the African invasion in 1942.

Lt. Walter Krozel, a U of R student who went through the CPT program, and his crew were waiting for clearance to taxi onto the runway to begin their 20th mission as part of an anti-submarine squadron whose primary objective was to destroy Nazi submarines wreaking havoc with Allied shipping.

Just as a British Lancaster bomber touched down, it suddenly ground-looped into the waiting B-24 Liberator bomber, and both planes blew up in a violent explosion.

Krozel's wife, Margaret, who was expecting their first child at the time, received a telegram from General "Hap" Arnold informing her that her husband had been killed in action and that information regarding burial arrangements would be forthcoming.

But a Red Cross volunteer in the British field hospital was puzzled over the identity of one of the survivors who mumbled incoherently about his son becoming a pilot. After 21 days, the error was discovered. It was the co-pilot who had been killed, not pilot Walt Krozel. Walt, though badly burned, was indeed alive.

Immediately telegrams were sent advising Margaret that Walt

was recovering in an American field hospital. Walt and Margaret celebrate their wedding anniversary on July 25, and their baby, a girl, is now a grandmother living in Hilton.

He spent the next six months recuperating. During his delirious 3 weeks, Walt said, he kept thinking that he wanted to see his son become a pilot. But the baby was a girl.

Walt returned to the States and was discharged. He spent the remainder of the war in the Rochester area, doing a little flying with Hylan but most of the time helping sell war bonds.

Many of Rochester's finest men never returned from the war. Casualties were extremely high. Capt. Sam Atlas, who served as a night fighter pilot with the Marine Corps on Guadalcanal, admitted losses were greater than 50 percent in his unit. Other reports stated that only 3 of 32 returned alive.

On April 1, 1944, the Army Air Corps had all the pilots, navigators and bombardiers it needed, and the war training service program here was terminated. That year, we built 86,000 planes (Ford Motor Co. at Willow Run, Ypsilanti, MI one every 55 minutes! 8,645 in all from 1943-45), 36,000 more than President Roosevelt had promised the American people a few years earlier.

Rochester as Communications Center

Little has been written about the importance of Rochester as a communications center in the complex airway network.

This city, being the last FAA radio range under the jurisdiction of Cleveland Airway Traffic Control, was a must-report point for all eastbound traffic prior to entering Boston's ATC jurisdiction 25 miles west of Syracuse.

Although it started in 1942 with a trickle of B-17s and B-24s, the load kept increasing as the months went by. In 1943 and 1944, occasionally 25 or 30 planes a day would report en route to various bases in New England.

But one extremely hot summer day in July 1944, when the number of flights peaked at 170, all planes were cleared over the area during a 90-minute period.

The planes, all of which maintained radio silence from their departure points (Lincoln, Nebraska; Grand Island, Nebraska; Salina, Kansas; and Albuquerque, New Mexico) first received their destination information from Rochester radio, as well as an ATC clearance from Boston.

They were cleared to either Dow Field, Bangor, Maine; Grenier Field, Manchester, New Hampshire; Presque Isle, Maine; and a few to Westover Field, Massachusetts. I often wondered how many crew members said, "I got my training right here in Rochester!"

Rochester has always been a great aviation city. Because the residents of Gates, Chili, and the 19th Ward were tolerant of some engine noise, it was these same planes and pilots provided us with the means to achieve final victory.

A few days following V-J Day in 1945, a pilot flying a C-87 from Fairbanks, Alaska, reported over Rochester. It was a routine transmission until the very end, when the pilot reported that the purpose of his mission was to "ferry snowballs from Alaska to Bermuda."

Rochester's Connection with the Tuskegee Airmen...

Aviation Cadet Louis Bracey, USAAF, at the Tuskegee Army Air Corps Flying School. He served overseas in Saipan and Okinawa.

He was one of my cadets in a short-lived, quasi-USAAF Civilian Pilot Training program in the fall of '42. A mere 61 years elapsed before we reconnected with each another.

This 1944 photo of Tom Cambisi shows his glider squadron in the background.

Kentucky Teenagers Guide Pilot to Safe Landing During World War II

The year was 1944. The Allies and the Axis powers were engaged in a global struggle to determine the future of mankind — whether we were to live as a free people or under the heels of dictators and despots.

Closer to home, the world took on a different hue. Although the war was made too vividly real by the breathstilling telegrams that afflicted family after family, life somehow managed to go on.

People still laughed, gossiped, and argued over the ump's calls for the local Triple A farm club of the St. Louis Cardinals. "Don't Sit Under the Apple Tree With Anyone Else But Me" was the latest hit from the Andrews Sisters. It was a big number on the juke boxes, at a nickel a play. A billboard near Scottsville Road read, "If necking is your sport, trade in your car for a davenport: Use Burma Shave."

"Racing With the Moon" was the theme song with which baritone Vaughn Monroe ended all his radio broadcasts. Monroe spent much of his time flying his Lockheed Lodestar from one military post to another, dispensing thousands of packs of cigarettes to the GIs. I can't recall which brand sponsored him. It was either "I'd Walk a Mile for a Camel" or "Not a Cough in a Carload."

Gen. Patton's 3rd Army was moving at breakneck speed across France with the Nazis on the run, but when gasoline supplies could no longer keep up with his advancing tanks, the drive came to a halt.

Around that time, Flight Officer Tom Cambisi was about to encounter a nerve-shattering event of his own. Cambisi, who had soloed at the Rochester Airport in 1931 at the age of 14 and trained with Gordy Root and Freddie McGinn at Page Airways, was no stranger to getting himself out of tight spots.

Like most intrepid pilots, Cambisi knew that this war was an all-or-nothing proposition and was willing to do whatever it took to defeat our foes. However, one night in particular would never fade from Cambisi's mind: October 8, 1944.

When asked years later to recall what had happened that dark fall night, he calmly replied, "Have a seat and I'll tell you one of the more heroic tales of World War II. That evening, I was deadheading as a passenger in the front cockpit of a PT-19, being flown by a rookie pilot as part of a three-plane group flying from Memphis, Tennessee, to Bowling Green, Kentucky. Final destination, North Carolina. But the lead pilot had neglected to pick up his sectional chart, and consequently all three planes were lost.

"You see, I had been on emergency leave to visit my sick mother in California. In the meantime, my outfit, which was commanded by Capt. Phil "Flip" Corcoran of 'Terry and the Pirates' fame shipped out to the Burma theater. Included in the contingent of the glider group was a flying buddy named Jackie Coogan, the former child movie star.

"Since I'd missed my outfit, I was transferred to another squadron being outfitted for service in Europe. On that fateful night, I was hitching cross-country from one Air Force base to another to my ultimate destination, Lauranberg, North Carolina.

"As darkness set in, all we could see were the silhouettes of the mountain tops, with total darkness below. At this point, I turned to the young aviator and yelled 'We'd better climb to 5,000, slow her down, and bail out!' The petrified young pilot replied, 'No! I can't jump. You take over.'

"I agreed, with one stipulation, 'Keep your hands and feet off the controls.' He readily agreed.

"I spotted a small town, which turned out to be Glasgow, Kentucky, and after I made several passes to alert the population that a plane was in trouble, dozens of headlights started appearing on a road, all congregating at a nearby airstrip. However, in the rush to assist us, the glare from the headlights blinded us instead,to the point that we couldn't make out anything on the ground.

"But then something peculiar happened. I spotted two flashlights, one stationary, the other rapidly moving away, then coming to an abrupt halt 400 feet away. The two people on the ground began waving the beams, indicating it was safe to land.

"I cautiously approached the field, spotted a small floodlight on a barn and a tree immediately adjacent to the barn. Fishtailing the plane, barely skimming over the barn, we touched down and headed for the flashlight at the far end of the field.

"At the last moment we cut the switch and ground-looped the plane, which was rapidly running out of space. The two of us raised our goggles, hopped out of the plane, and started to unbuckle our parachutes when the person who had so miraculously guided us to a safe landing yelled, 'Are you hurt?'

"There in the pitch black field stood a brave little 12-year-old-girl, half-frightened to death. We were dumbfounded — our lives had been saved by two sisters, one 12, the other 14, who lived with their widowed mother. They alone had the wisdom to outline the usable landing area, thus paving the way for a safe emergency landing.

"The local citizenry arrived next, eager to help. Practically every American family at that time had someone in the service, and the motto of 'cooperation' bound friends, families, and strangers as one.

"The two sisters and their mother invited me and the student pilot to join them in a late evening snack and to spend the night, an offer we gratefully accepted.

"The following morning, the whole town turned out to witness our departure. Less than 400 feet of space was available for takeoff. I set the flaps on the PT-19 to 10 degrees, had some men hold the wings while I revved up my 175-hp Ranger engine to 1600 rpm, then signaled to let go.

"I quickly pushed the stick forward to get the tail off the ground and opened the throttle all the way. As the plane gained speed, I eased back on the control stick and gently lifted off, barely clearing the fence by a few feet at the end of the field.

"I then stuck the nose down, picked up air speed, and started a climbing turn, leveling off at about 700 feet. I banked and stuck the nose down while leaving the throttle open and zoomed over the spectators below doing at least 120 mph. What a roar it must have made.

"Although I had learned the names of the two sisters, I regrettably lost the slip of paper somewhere overseas. I was assigned to the glider squadron, flying a Waco CG-4A glider (nicknamed the 'American Kamikaze'). Then, in an operation in the vicinity of the Rhine River, my glider was disabled by anti-aircraft fire. I was able to successfully ride the craft down but injured my back in the crash, pains I still feel today.

"In 1986, 42 years after that fateful night in 1944, my wife and I returned to Glasgow, Kentucky, where I had the chance to discuss my experience with a reporter from the Glasgow *Daily Times*. After the story was published, two women contacted me — Laura Wade McCoy and Ruby Wade, the two little girls who had made such a great and brave contribution in saving the lives of two World War II pilots.

"A joyous reunion was held, during which we all celebrated this remarkable feat by children courageous beyond their young years. God bless them!"

A Piece of Aviation History from Dansville, New York
by Louise Molyneux

Lynn Pickard, resident of Dansville, NY, was bitten by the flying bug in 1911 when Walter Johnson landed a Thomas Headless biplane in a field north of the village. Pickard flew in World War I and then barnstomed around the country in the 1920's. Pickard went on to establish the airport in Dansville which was dedicated on October 1-2, 1927. During the Great Depression federal funding provided paved runways, lighting, and a hangar to improve he airport. During World War II, Pickard headed a flight school which trained a contingent of Naval Cadets. They were housed at the P.C. (Physical Culture) Hotel in Dansville as well as in student housing in Geneseo. Their flight lessons were in Piper Cubs at the Dansville Airport and ground school was at the college in Geneseo. David and Donald Molyneux were cadets in this program and David's wife Barbara reports that they received two years of college credit for this work. On may 19, 1975 the airport was officially renamed Dansville Municipal Airport – Pickard Field.

Eight Piper Cubs, owned by US Navy, used for training Naval Cadets. Photo courtesy of Captain Jon Vanderhoof, USAF. (1943)

Naval Cadets marching Memorial Day in Dansville. Photo courtesy of Captain Jon Vanderhoof, USAF. (1943)

High Above Normandy

On June 6, 1944, the Allied world watched and waited as 156,000 American, British and Canadian troops landed on the beaches of Normandy.

Just prior to the invasion, Gen. Eisenhower told his forces, "You are about to embark upon a great crusade." Among the 1,347 fighter planes, 1,350 heavy bombers, 426 B-26s, 1,613 gliders towed by C-47s, and 1,140 planeloads of paratroopers (which flew a total of 7,106 sorties) were several Rochesterians who participated in this pivotal battle for freedom.

Because I was a civilian pilot during the war years, I never flew combat missions or personally experienced the hazards of warfare. What follows are the accounts of several military pilots, which I hope will provide a sense of immediacy to air combat during World War II. These are the stories of men who had yet to see their 25th birthday, who knew that their fight to save the world from Hitler could mean they might never return to their families or loved ones.

Bernie Newmark

Bombing Runs and Nightmares

By May of 1944, Captain Bernie Newmark was among a select few pilots who had been overseas risking their lives on the front lines of the air for nearly a full tour. At the time, a tour was 25 missions, and, though the odds were against surviving so many missions, some were making it.

Every so often, there were rumors of an invasion of Europe. Three or four times, there had been actual alerts when everything shifted to a high state of readiness. Leaves were cancelled, and all pilots and support personnel were ordered immediately back to their bases. But all of the alerts had turned out to be false alarms.

"At the time, we were on Cromher Road in Norwich, at Horsham

St. Faith, which was like Brighton in relationship to Rochester," Newmark recalled.

"It was about then that our tours were increased to 30 missions, and then to 35. They shipped many of us off to 'flak houses' for R&R. These were large manor houses where we could wear casual clothes, play baseball or touch football, ride bikes around the countryside, or do just about anything we wanted, only dressing in uniforms for dinner. This was all supposed to help us get rid of the jitters."

But for those who had exceeded 20 missions, the new minimums were like a chapter out of *Catch 22*, disheartening and discouraging, to say the least. They'd been lucky to reach 20 and understandably wanted to finish their tours and return to the States.

"In hindsight," he noted, "we realized this was calculated to keep some of the more experienced crews around for the real thing.

"At the base on the day before D-Day, I wrote home wondering if the invasion would ever come off."

In early June, at a flak house in southern England near the Bournemouth coast, they saw so many troops they imagined England sinking from their weight.

That night, there was another alert, which Newmark and his colleagues assumed was another false alarm. Until about 2 in the morning, when everyone was rousted from their bunks and ordered to the operations room.

"This was the real thing! We were shown the maps and told our positions. The 754th Squadron, 458th Group was to hit the landing beaches six minutes before the troops. Our job was to come in over their heads as they came ashore. We had to make sure we didn't drop short on the landing boats or drop long on the paratroopers already there."

Newmark was deputy lead of the wing for the radar plane, nicknamed the "Mickey." Because they would be reaching the Normandy beaches in the dark, his plane would take over if the Mickey didn't make it.

"We were told to fly shuttles as long as necessary. We returned to the base, refueled, reloaded and waited for takeoff orders, sleeping on the tarmac under the wings. A few hours later, we made a second trip, then a third. When the weather set in, we slept under the wings again. This went on for 56 hours!"

The pilots and crews were given "alertness" pills (most likely caffeine or Benzedrine), and Newmark still has what's left of his. "I'm not sure how alert we were," he observed, "but we had nightmares for the next few days. I wrote home when we finally got back to our beds, and some of what I wrote is totally incoherent."

Lt. Charles Steinberg, England, 1944

D-Day False Alarms

Lt. Charles Steinberg was aviation ordinance and bomb disposal officer for the 586th Bombardment Squadron, which flew Martin B-26 Marauders, twin-engine planes that carried a two-ton payload. Depending on weather, Marauders could fly 4 to 5 hours at up to 250 mph. Because Steinberg also was rated as an aerial gunner, he later was designated squadron gunnery officer.

"We arrived in England in February 1944 and were operational early in March," he remembered. "Our major targets were bridges, rail yards, fuel dumps, and mysterious targets that looked like toboggan slides and turned out to be launch platforms for the pilotless bombs the Germans used after June 6, 1944."

Around May 15, Steinberg and some 20 other officers were summoned to Command Headquarters, where they were briefed on the D-Day invasion. All they were told about the date was that it would be the day after they were ordered to prepare 250-pound bombs with instantaneous nose fuses.

"Sure enough," Steinberg recalled, "on the afternoon of June 4, the field order came down. We loaded each of the 12 bombers in my squadron with 16 bombs, and I fused them with instantaneous fuses."

But no sooner had they finished the job than the mission was aborted, which meant Steinberg had to defuse the 192 bombs, unload them, and store them away from the bombers.

"On June 5, we got the same order again, and we repeated the loading and fusing, but with more haste, since we were scheduled for a briefing at 2:15 am on the 6th, with takeoff set for 4:15 am. But by takeoff, the weather was terrible, with a heavy fog bank down to about 200 feet."

The bombers took off on schedule, but while forming up, two planes collided and all 12 crew members were killed, one of them, T. Sgt. Edward Monaghan, a gunner from Rochester.

On the way to their target in Verreville, France, one of the B-26s iced up over England and, as it plunged downward, crashed into a bomber below it. Only one of the 12 crew members managed to bail out.

"Our target was a gun position about a quarter-mile inland from Omaha Beach. The bomb run was classified 'excellent' — 34 planes from my group dropped nearly 70 tons of bombs, and all the remaining planes returned to base before 8 am.

"As soon as they landed, we had to reload them for a run at another gun position, at Benerville, also near Omaha Beach, that same afternoon."

A number of ground personnel had snuck aboard planes for the historic invasion, but Steinberg wasn't among them because he was sleeping off the exhausting work of the previous 48 hours. He didn't get to see the invasion beaches until two weeks later while a crew member on a bombing run on the port of Le Havre.

"By the time we were over the city, the smoke from earlier attacks rose up over 8,000 feet."

Lt. Richard Warboys poses with his plane in September 1944.

A Bird's Eye View of the Longest Day

Lt. Richard Warboys recalled that rumors of an invasion of Europe had been circulating for quite a while when all leaves were cancelled on Sunday, May 29, 1944. The mood became more intense as orders were issued that all personnel were to wear sidearms at all times.

During the following days, his group performed routine missions, but on Sunday, June 5, Warboys was assigned to the late alert watch.

"This consisted of four P-47s sitting on the end of the runway with engines running, ready for a fast scramble in case of an enemy air attack," he noted. "At dark, we left the planes for coffee and sleep. At 1:30 am, we were awakened by a loud blast near our base, which turned out to be a British Bren Carrier that blew up while in a convoy. 'Boy, oh boy, we're being invaded!' we thought."

At 2 am, the information officer advised them of a briefing in 45 minutes. When they arrived at the flight line, every P-47 was painted with battle stripes. It was then that they knew something big was about to happen.

"At the briefing, Col. "Hub" Zemke announced, 'This is it. The day we've been waiting for — D-Day.' He filled us in on what had been happening — the landing barges crossing the Channel, the Navy blasting away at the Normandy coast, and our troops landing at five beachheads.

"The 61st and 63rd squadrons were to fly the first mission,with "Gaby" Gabreski leading us. At 0325 hours, we took off for Ostend, Belgium, with only our wing lights on. Our mission was to intercept any enemy planes coming out of Holland to counterattack the beachheads."

No enemy planes were sighted, but the Germans jammed their radio transmissions by counting from 1 to 10 and back, in German, and threatening, "Come over! Good food, good beds, good treatment! Otherwise, *Death, Death, Death!*" They were forced to listen to the psychological propaganda for 4 hours and then landed at 8:10 am.

At 9:55 am, they began their next mission, this time led by Russ Westfall, their operations officer. The 16-plane group dive-bombed bridges and strafed troop convoys and any road and rail traffic. They completed that mission at 12:20 pm.

At 5 pm, the 63rd Squadron Commander, Capt. Goodfleisch, asked Warboys if he would fly a relay mission. The beachhead commanders were receiving broken radio transmissions from London and needed a relay point.

"My job was to fly up to 32,000 feet where I could clearly pick up the transmissions and then fly up and down the Channel just off the French coast, repeating the messages to the ground commanders.

"I had a real bird's eye view of the invasion. I could see both sides of the smoke screen the Navy was laying down. On the one side, I could see the landing barges heading for France and the battleships firing their big guns. On the other side, I could see the battered wrecks of the invasion fleet wallowing in the water while the Germans fired on the landing troops.

"This colossal undertaking to preserve the free world was a sight I'll never forget. I finally landed for the day at 2100 hours — a long, long day."

Invisible Targets

Roy Beaney

As a 21-year-old B-24 pilot in the 8th Air Force stationed at Rakheath Air Force Base west of Norwich, England, Capt. Roy Beaney wasn't surprised when, on June 3, 1944, the 96th Wing, 467 Bomber Group, and the 790th Squadron were placed on alert and ordered confined to their base.

Under cover of darkness in the early hours of June 6, the 12 planes in Beaney's group took off, formed up, and proceeded across the Channel. At 9000 feet, about halfway across, they got the first glimpse of daybreak, though it was still dark below in England and France. Beaney's plane was the deputy lead, and the other bombers in the group got their orders by Morse code transmitted by a light on the tail of the lead plane.

"At this point, considerable confusion developed," Beaney recalled. "Planes from other squadrons drifted into our formation to decipher the code, while some of our planes got entangled with other bombers. Remember, there were several thousand Allied planes involved in the operation.

"Through the breaks in the clouds, we could see huge balls of fire and saw that the battleship *Texas* had been unfortunately hit by one of our own misplaced bombs. The landing craft looked like small water bugs, and the most awesome sight were the hundreds of P-47s (known as "Jugs") and P-51s that virtually blackened the sky."

As they neared France, they switched to the GEE Box to guide them to their target. The box was a British invention, which allowed pilots to program target coordinates by degrees, minutes and seconds of latitude and longitude.

"We were headed for Port-en-Bessin, France. We had a gauge on

49

our instrument panel that had two hands. When they were at right angles to each other, it indicated we were within a quarter of a mile of our target — whether we could see it or not."

After completing a six-hour run, the group refueled and returned to France on another mission. All the planes returned safely, and not a single Nazi plane got near the bombers during the entire operation.

"All told, I flew 35 missions in Europe. This was a far cry from the time I was a 16-year-old apprentice working at Hylan Airport in exchange for free flight lessons in a 37-hp Piper Cub!"

My Fair Lady*

The Statue of Liberty as viewed from the co-pilot's window of a B-17. Aircraft to the right is a B-24. Photo courtesy of Capt. Jerry Osadnick.

*Last line of childhood ditty: "London Bridge is Falling Down."

Like Coming Out of a Dream

Major Elmer Pankratz

The weather was fine as Elmer Pankratz flew his third tactical reconnaissance mission. He was number two man in a group of P-51 Mustangs flying in pairs. His job was to keep watch for flak or German aircraft so the group leader could concentrate on the ground.

Pankratz remembered, "We'd been told if you gave a good German flak crew 30 seconds of straight, level flying, there was a good chance you'd be nailed. So as we approached the mission area, we began 'jinking' — constantly weaving and changing altitude."

Pankratz had enjoyed acrobatics during training and had never felt queasy. So jinking was no problem — until that day.

"It wasn't long before my stomach said, 'Hey, I'm not enjoying this! If you don't quit, I'll make you regret it!'"

But he had to keep weaving while watching the sky. "And sure enough, my stomach went into reverse. Which was no big deal except that I had my oxygen mask on. We were low enough that I didn't need oxygen, but my microphone was part of the mask. And I needed the mike in place to immediately warn my No. 1 of any danger. This was no fun."

He decided to fly straight and level, just gently weaving until they encountered any enemy fire, hoping he wasn't over a sharp flak crew.

"During the next 32 missions, enemy fire came close four times, and you never saw a more violent display of jinking. There was no time to get sick."

Pankratz didn't recall feeling any strong emotions when V-E Day finally came, "just a strange feeling like coming out of a dream."

51

"Any good feelings were doused because we soon learned about half the squadron was slated for Japan. And I was on the list.

"I'm one guy who applauded the decision to drop the A-bomb," Pankratz said. "It was long past the time to end the business of trying to stay alive while doing your duty and getting to the business of enjoying life again."

Homeward Bound

Between July 1944 and April 1945, Harold Ehrlich flew a B-24 with the 15th Air Force out of Italy. After his 35th and final mission at the end of April, he was ordered back to the States.

"I had mixed emotions," he recalled. "I was anxious to get home but knew I would miss the camaraderie of the bomber group.

"We boarded the *SS Mariposa* in Naples on May 1st. This was my first trip aboard a ship, so I didn't know what to expect. The bunk-bed quarters were crowded, but I thought the food was good. Cruising through the Mediterranean was peaceful. The water was blue and calm, and the sun was shining. Being aboard a troop ship didn't seem too bad."

But once the *Mariposa* passed Gibraltar and headed into the Atlantic, Ehrlich began noticing the effect of the swells. The first few days weren't too bad, but when weather got worse, the ship's movements became more violent.

He noticed attendance in the dining room declining. "And by the fourth day out, I was constantly in my bunk trying to persuade my stomach that everything was OK — just mind over matter.

"As things got worse and I wondered why anyone would join the Navy, news of V-E Day arrived. But the good news didn't help my physical feelings one bit. My condition didn't improve until we approached New York Harbor and passed the Statue of Liberty. By then, my only wish was to disembark and walk on firm ground again!"

Accolades to the Andrews Sisters

It was a dark and stormy night that time back in March 1943, when Cleveland Airway Traffic Control Center called Boston Airway Traffic, and I was monitoring both sides of the conversation:

CLE: I have an inbound…

BOS: "Shoot"

CLE: Air Force 8136, B-24 enroute Louisville, to Dorval Field Montreal, at 9,000 estimating crossing Red Airway 23, vicinity Bath, NY at 2139E

BOS: Repeat the name of the town in New York

CLE: Bath, New York

BOS: Can't make it out, spell it please.

CLE: B-A-T-H

BOS: Sorry, still don't understand you.

CLE: *In desperation:* Bath. What do you take on Saturday night?

BOS: *After a 5 second pause:* 'rum and coca-cola..'

(Perhaps I should explain, many years ago, children were always given a bath on Saturday nights.)

Top: (left to right) Lt. Rossitor Mikel, Lt. Joe Kiseleski, Lt. Robert Laut; Bottom: Cpl. George Maiden, Cpl. Jack Waters, Cpl. Lloyd Klute

Air Combat Memories

Joseph Kiseleski was accepted into the Air Force Aviation Cadet program in the fall of 1942. The following January, he was assigned to Atlantic City for basic training.

"The actor Broderick Crawford was an aide to our company commander," he recalls. After classification, our initial flight training was at Carlstrom Field, Florida."

He went through basic engine training at Courtland, Alabama, and advanced twin-engine training at Freeman Field, Indiana, where he was awarded his wings, given his pilot status, and commissioned as a second lieutenant in February 1944.

His B-25 training was at Greenville Air Base, South Carolina, followed by operational training at Muroc, California — now Edwards Air Force Base. From there, he shipped to Seattle, Washington, for the trip to Hawaii, where he was assigned to the 7th Air Force, 41st Bomb Group, 47th Bomb Squadron at Wheeler Field.

"Our group had done considerable damage to the Japanese at several South Seas islands and had returned to Hawaii to rest and regroup for further action.

"We formed a small group of eight B-25s, with crews, to provide navigational escort for fighter planes to be based at more distant islands such as Guam, Tinian, and Saipan. Sometimes, we had P-47s, other times P-51s, all to be used for the B-29 raids against Japan. We did these flights through Johnson Majuro, and Eniwetok and occasionally flew to Japanese-held Truk on harassment missions.

When his squadron went to Leyte in the Philippines, his group was ordered to join them there. On their flight from Tinian to Peleliu, their B-25 developed engine problems but they arrived safely. The plane was repaired, and they flew on to Leyte.

"This wasn't to be an easy trip," he remembers. "About one hour from Peleliu, flying at 8,000 feet and without any warning, both engines quit. We thought we would have to ditch, but we managed to get the engines restarted. Miraculously, the incident only cost us a few thousand feet of altitude. But the repair station condemned the plane, given its recent history.

Fortunately, Kiseleski bumped into a former cadet friend who was flying a C-47 to Leyte. He agreed to take the crew with him, but because of the delays, their squadron by then had moved on to Moratoi, and they had to hitch another ride to rejoin them. After a short stay there, they moved on to Okinawa.

"At war's end, we expected to return to the States, but I was transferred to the Fifth Air Force P-51 fighter squadron at Osaka, Japan. I had the chance to fly a Canadian Northlander over Nagasaki, which had been devastated by the second atom bomb. I flew over a destroyed Mitsubishi factory, which had built many of the 'Zeros.'

"I stayed at the Fifth Air Force Headquarters in Tokyo and even toured the emperor's summer palace in Kyoto. Despite the many hazards of World War II combat, I'm left with many good memories of the camaraderie of our Air Force experience."

A Successful Aborted Mission

In late October 1944, David Taschman and his crew were
scheduled to lead a wing of several hundred B-17 Flying Fortresses
on a bomb run at a target in southeastern Germany. They took
off at 5 am and rendezvoused with the other planes. Their
estimated time of arrival at the target was 7:30 am.

Though they were the lead plane, their pilot suddenly advised
his crew that he couldn't get enough power to reach their bombing
altitude of 30,000 feet.

Taschman recalls, "We flew on for a bit, and he told me to
jettison 17 of our 20-bomb payload to see if we could maintain our
climb with only 750 lbs of bombs on board.

"We did as ordered but still couldn't get over 20,000 feet.
Reluctantly, we turned over command of the mission to the back-up
plane and headed back to base in Foggia, Italy. On the way back, we
saw a moving train in northern Hungary."

The pilot suggested dropping the three remaining bombs on the
train, and Taschman asked him to turn so they were headed in the
same direction as the train. The pilot cautioned that the train might
have anti-aircraft guns aboard, and the maneuver could give them
time to aim at the bomber.

"So, I dropped my three remaining bombs, aiming perpendicular to
the center of the train. They fell just a few feet short, and we turned
and raced home since we were unescorted and feared attack by
German fighters."

When the crews that had flown on to the original target returned several hours later, they reported that the concussion from
Taschman's bomb drop had derailed the train. "So, we actually
got credit for our aborted mission!"

1st Lt. David Taschman, USAAF.
Navigator & Bombardier
Photo as an Aviation Cadet.

(Group Photo)
Lt. Taschman, Rear Row, 1st on left.

Flying Errors: The Bane of Pilots

Lt. Col. Colin Storey

Lt. Col. Colin Storey recalls that, when he was a young aviation cadet in flight school during World War II, one of the most dreaded things that could befall a pilot was a "check ride," a kind of blot on your record, which cast doubt on a flyer's abilities. Many aviators were washed out by these examination rides.

"I was no stranger to flying errors myself," Storey noted, "and I got my check ride during primary flight school in Douglas, Georgia, where I had just soloed in a PT-17, an open cockpit biplane that was the primary trainer."

Storey and his instructor, also in a PT-17, were using an auxiliary field, about 20 miles from the main field.

"I was the last cadet to solo that late in the day. Since all flying stopped at dusk, my instructor told me to fly back to the home field."

As Storey took off, he looked back and saw his instructor also taking off but headed in the opposite direction.

"I thought it was strange that he would fly off in the wrong direction. But after about 10 minutes, I realized the field was nowhere in sight and it suddenly dawned on me that it was *me* who was flying the wrong way! I was lost and had no radio equipment!"

He made three 90-degree turns and eventually wound up back at the auxiliary field where he'd soloed. Though it was against the rules to land without an instructor on the field, he decided to land and get his bearings.

"After I landed, I recalled I'd once practiced landings at the same field with my instructor and, on our final take-off, he'd taken off downwind, held the plane on the ground as we raced towards the trees at the end of the field, and then pulled up and cleared them at the last possible second. I'd been impressed with that feat and now decided to duplicate it myself."

Once airborne, Storey realized he was finally headed back to his home field. On the way, he passed three PT-17s headed in the opposite direction.

"I landed, and as I parked, I saw the squadron commander standing waiting for me."

He wanted to know why Storey was late and if he'd gotten lost. In fact, the commander had assumed that was the case and had sent out the three planes to search for Storey.

"I knew if I admitted I'd been lost I was in for a check ride, so I said I had just lost track of time while practicing my aerial acrobatics."

Fortunately, the commander accepted the tale but ordered him to write "I will keep track of the time while practicing my acrobatic flying" 500 times and to turn it in the next day.

He had come close to washing out, but Storey's white lie had saved him from a dreaded termination of his pilot training.

A Near Catastrophe in a B-17

Probably the most famous bomber of World War II was the renowned B-17 Flying Fortress. But Colin Storey recalls that the plane actually got off to a shaky start during its initial flight for the Army Air Corps in the 1930s.

"Both the plane and crew were lost when the B-17 crashed on takeoff at Wright Air Force Base in Dayton, Ohio, a tragedy in itself and a setback for Boeing, which lost the contract to Lockheed as a result."

An investigation revealed the crash was caused by a failure to unlock the flight controls before takeoff, a tragic lesson learned by many pilots who failed to run through their check-off list.

Storey notes, "I can personally relate to that lesson since I made the same mistake prior to my first combat mission in a B-17 with the 94th Bomb Group, 8th Air Force in England on December 23, 1944.

That morning, the Group experienced several delays at the outset of a 36-plane bombing mission to Kaiserlautern, Germany.

"I was 30th in line for take off. But by the time I reached the end of the runway, the Group was running very late. I was used to taxiing the B-17 with its controls locked to prevent the vertical tail controls from flapping in the wind and vibrating the control column. My usual procedure was to line up on the take-off runway, lock the brakes, rev up the four Wright Cyclone engines to full power, unlock the controls, release the brakes, and head down the runway."

But on this particular morning, Storey got the green light from the control tower the moment he swung onto the runway. As the plane sped towards takeoff, his co-pilot called out their increasing speed. But as they reached take-off speed, about three-quarters down the runway, Storey pulled back on the control column and immediately realized it was still locked.

"The locking mechanism was on the floor between me and the co-pilot and required two hands to release it. We were approaching the end of the runway, and I had no time to alert my co-pilot or to abort. So I reached down with my right hand, pulled on the mechanism as hard as I could, and fortunately it released.

"The plane lifted, cleared the trees, and we were on our way with an 8,000-pound bomb load. Had the lock not released, we would have crashed into the trees at the end of the field, and the plane and its bombs would have exploded, killing 10 crewman."

It was a mistake Colin Storey never made again.

From Here to Infantry To Airforce
(the hard way)

Lt. Charles R. Witmer, USAF, a Combat Flight Leader of an RF-86 Squadron during the Korean War, became a pilot via an unorthodox and challenging route.

On December 6, 1944, at the age of 17, he enlisted in the Corps of Engineers and soon became a Pfc. Because of a strong background in both math and physics, he was sent to Virginia Military Institute (VMI) for one year but squeezed two years of training into just the one year because they were his favorite subjects. In 1947, he was accepted as a plebe at the United States Military Academy at West Point and commissioned as a 2nd Lt. in 1951. Among his classmates were "Buzz" Aldrin, the second man to land on the moon behind Neil Armstrong. He completed his flight training in 1952 and was sent to Korea as a photo reconnaissance pilot.

Lt. Charles R. Witmer Jr.

Following his discharge from the Air Force, Lt. Witmer assumed an engineering position with Eastman Kodak Company.

Although many of his "spy" missions were in the 40-45K range, he managed to keep "both feet on the ground"...

Charles R. Witmer Jr., Sam T. Dickens, and Frank Halstead, all 1st Lt. USAF

Doolittle's Raid Rallied the Nation

General James Doolittle

A letter to the editor of Gannett Rochester papers decrying the fact that the death of Gen. James Doolittle wasn't covered on the front page had some justification.

Between December 7, 1941, the date of the infamous attack on Pearl Harbor, and April 18, 1942, when Radio Tokyo announced Japan was being bombed by American B-25s, our nation had precious little to cheer about.

Almost all the news was somber and gloomy — retreat after retreat — with the exception of some daring bombing missions in the Pacific by Capt. Colin Kelly, a B-17 pilot. One of his crew members, bombardier Sgt. Meyer Levin, spent a good part of his youth on Woodbury Street in Rochester. Sadly, in a subsequent raid, the entire crew perished.

On April 18, Jimmy Doolittle (who had a doctorate from Massachusetts Institute of Technology) led a group of 16 B-25 bombers from the deck of the aircraft carrier *USS Hornet* on a daring raid over Tokyo. Although the bombing results were not all that spectacular, the raid itself immediately began restoring national confidence that we were fighting back and that ultimate victory would be ours.

In February 1945, Captain Joseph Clemow of Rochester was transferred from the Army Air Corps Ferry and Test Flying Service at Warton Air Depot near Preston, Lancashire, England, to Loges Field in St. Germain — a Paris suburb. There, he was assigned to Gen. Carl "Tooey" Spaatz to fly a small twin-engine Beechcraft C-45 for operating in small airports on short trips.

On March 2, 1945, he flew Gens. Spaatz and Doolittle from

Rheims, France, to Liege, Belgium and back. On March 17, he flew Gens. Spaatz, Doolittle and Vandenburg from South Central France to Namur, Belgium and back. On April 1, he flew General Doolittle from Paris to London, and on April 10 from Rheims to Paris.

On some flights Gen. Doolittle would do the piloting, but he usually spent the time with other generals planning bombing or strafing missions. This was a satisfying experience for Joe, who, after the war, served as chief pilot for Eastman Kodak for 30 years.

After the war, Jimmy Doolittle became president of the Space Technology Laboratories of TRW Corp. and also served as a board member of the parent company. A Pittsford, New York, resident, Capt. Cyril "Cy" Noon served as a test pilot in the Air Force during the war and then became director of engineering at TRW. In Cleveland, Cy became acquainted with Jimmy Doolittle and spent many hours with him over the years.

In Cy's own words "Jimmy loved to tell stories and was an expert at it. We talked about the Tokyo raid and many other interesting and thrilling episodes. One that particularly sticks in my mind involved Jimmy demonstrating Curtiss airplanes in South America.

"It was in the interest of the Army for Curtiss to get foreign orders so that its airplane factories would be healthier. Jimmy was on leave from the Army in 1926 to demonstrate Curtiss airplanes in Chile. The competition was fierce, with the best pilots from Germany, Italy, and Great Britain showing off their aeronautical wares.

"A party was held one evening on the second floor of the hotel where they were staying, and Jimmy was mimicking the then – popular swashbuckling movie actor, Douglas Fairbanks, by walking on his hands. The hand-walking continued on out to the balcony where a rail broke and dropped Jimmy 20 feet to the ground below, breaking both his legs below the knees.

"The following morning, with heavy casts on each leg, he was hoisted into the cockpit where he proceeded to demonstrate his airplane and win the competition. He was able to continue the tour and won other sales for Curtiss in South America!"

This and other incidents are recounted in a book on Doolittle by renowned newscaster Lowell Thomas and Edward Jablonski.

The passing of such a hero, a true legend in his own time, should have received prominent recognition rather than a minor article buried inside one of the city's daily papers.

MEMBERS OF THE 61ST AND 63RD SQUADRON OF COL. GABRESKI'S FAMOUS 8TH AIR FORCE GROUP OXTED FIELD, COLCHESTER, ENGLAND — JULY 1944

Standard Operating Procedure for P-47 Instrument Approach
..1. Fly over "Cone of Silence"
..2. Toss Brick Overboard
..3. Follow Brick Down in Tight Formation

Ken Williams is probably the only World War II pilot to shoot himself down.

Remembering V-E Day

When our nation observed the 50th anniversary of the unconditional surrender of the German armies, it was appropriate to salute those men and women whose unflinching courage against great odds helped bring that phase of World War II to a successful close.

Here are the stories of some of their experiences and what they were doing on V-E (Victory in Europe) Day.

Ken Williams was a P-47 Thunderbolt pilot with the 355th Fighter Group in England who was selected to fly with Col. Glen Duncan, whose squadron acquired the nickname of "Bill's Buzz Boys."

Their mission was to develop tactics and techniques for low-level attacks on German airfields.

In March 1944, while leading an attack on a German airfield near Paris, he saw a light twin-engine bomber being serviced by a refueling truck. One quick burst, and the plane and truck blew up, and Ken had the dubious distinction of shooting himself down in the process, crashing about two miles beyond the air field.

Crawling from the wreckage, he ran into some adjacent woods and spent the next two days playing hide-and-seek with German troops.

At the end of the second day, tired, cold and scared, he saw three women walking along a path.

The youngest one, whose name was Suzanne, spoke excellent English and convinced her two aunts to bring him to their home. The aunts altered some clothes from a recently deceased uncle, and the following morning Suzanne and Ken caught a train for Paris.

Some weeks passed before Ken could connect with the French Underground and escape. In the meantime, his name was changed to Jean Tanguy, a 17-year-old farmer from Brittany, false ID papers were furnished, and he quickly acquired a respectable knowledge of French.

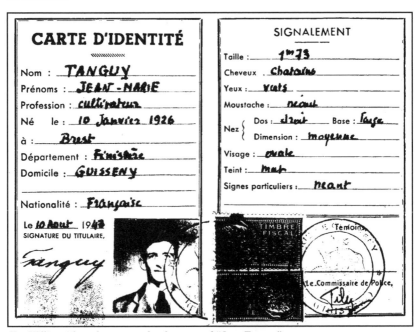

Ken Williams' forged papers under the name of "Jean Tanguy."

With the help of British officers, the night finally arrived for the trip back to England. It was almost 3 am when two black rubber rafts hit the beach. Williams quickly jumped into one and was soon climbing aboard a British PT boat. They were challenged by German "E" boats, and because one of the three engines on the British craft failed, they could not outrun the Germans. A running fight began, and Ken's boat took several hits, killing a British sailor manning one of the gun turrets. But two hours later, he was back on British soil.

One year after this escapade was V-E Day. Ken was stationed at West Hampton Beach, Long Island, going through an instructor gunnery program. On V-E Day, Ken and two fellow pilots decided to go into New York City to celebrate. One of the men in the party thought it would be fun to stop at every bar on the right-hand side of the road. Not sure of the distance to New York or how many bars were on the right side, needless to say they never got to the city. But celebrate they did.

Those of World War II vintage may remember the WASPs — not the "White-Anglo-Saxon-Protestant" type but the "Women's Air Force Service Pilots" type. They ferried wartime airplanes, did a lot of test flying, and towed target sleeves behind planes so fighter pilots and gunners in bombers and anti-aircraft batteries could practice shooting at a moving target.

Writing in the *Democrat and Chronicle* in 1977, Bill Beeney noted: "It was long before the era of women's lib, but there was a fair-sized contingent of women — 1,074 successfully completed training for quasi-military service during World War II."

June Bent, 1944

June Braun Bent was brought up in Des Moines, Iowa, attended Drake University and learned to fly, soloing in May 1940. Her husband, Jack, was a P-40 pilot in Africa.

In 1943, the WASP program got under way, and June was accepted for training in Sweetwater, Texas. Upon graduation, having earned her silver wings, she was assigned to the Air Force Basic Training School at Merced, California. With her engineering background, she was assigned to test BT-13s, a basic trainer that had been grounded for various malfunctions. Her job was to determine if it was airworthy for training operations.

In her own words: "My husband always tells everyone that he picked me up in a chow line. That's not quite correct.

"A few days after my arrival at Merced Air Force Base, California, a WASP friend and I were eating lunch at the Officer's Club when a pilot came up to our

Captain John Bent, June's husband

table and asked if he could join us. This man turned out to be Capt. John T. Bent, a P-40 pilot who had recently returned from service in North Africa and had been assigned to Merced as assistant intelligence officer.

"We dated after that, just like in the movies, and when John was reassigned to Minter Field, I flew him down. I think he was lonely, since he didn't know anyone at Minter, and I soon began getting letters. The upshot of it was we were married after knowing each other just $2^1/_2$ months, and the pianist playing at our 10-minute wedding reception was none other than RPO Pops guest conductor, Skitch Henderson, a P-40 pilot with the Royal Air Force in Africa."*

June remained in the WASPs until her deactivation on December 20, 1944. Because John had sufficient points, he was released from active duty in the spring of 1945 and accepted a position with Eastman Kodak at Kingsport, Tennessee, where they were living on V-E Day.

A Veteran's 15 Minutes of Fame
During World War II

Shortly after the Allied forces recaptured Manila in February 1945, Lt. Raymond Koehler of Penfield, a C-46 pilot with the 54th Troop Carrier Wing, 5th Air Force, 6th Combat Cargo Squadron, got the "15 minutes of fame" artist Andy Warhol predicted for all of us.

A graduate of Monroe High School's Class of 1939, Ray joined the Air Force in the fall of 1942 and became a pilot in June of 1944.

One day at Clark Field in the Philippines, Ray's plane was first in line to taxi onto the runway when his co-pilot said, "I think we've got a problem."

"Now what?" responded Ray. The co-pilot answered, "General MacArthur and a couple of his aides are approaching the tail of our plane."

Ray realized that the blast from the 2,000 horsepower engines would whip up a storm of dirt, sand, and whatever else directly at the three officers. So he wisely chose to hold his position.

The control tower advised him to taxi onto the runway and told him he would be No. 1 for takeoff. Ray didn't budge and held his position.

Moments later, the tower controller barked: "Taxi onto the runway immediately. There are four planes behind you waiting to take off." Bear in mind there were still some very fierce battles being fought with the Japanese in the Philippines.

Ray then complied with the tower's orders, gunning the outboard engine of his C-46 and making a 45-degree turn onto the runway. He looked around to see Gen. MacArthur and the two aides chasing their hats down the field. The blast from the propeller indeed had blown their hats away. Ray wasted no time taking off for his destination — Peleliu in the Palau Islands.

Ray had some other experiences that brought him into contact with celebrities. Upon entering the service, he was assigned to the Air Force Classification Center in Atlantic City, New Jersey. His drill sergeant was none other than that famous movie actor who starred in many movies and radio and TV series after the war — Broderick Crawford.

On another occasion, he arrived at a base in the South Pacific and a shiny new, highly polished Marine Corps C-46 pulled up alongside his plane at the ramp. A jeep approached and took both pilots to the Officer's Club. As Ray was about to depart following his lunch, the clearance officer asked, "Did you get his autograph?"

"Whose autograph?" Ray asked.

"The pilot with the beard who came in on the jeep with you," the officer said. "That was Tyrone Power!"

Perhaps the most unusual mission Ray flew was on New Year's Eve 1945, when a very special cargo was loaded onto his C-46 for transport from Tokyo to Osaka. Specific instructions were to attempt as smooth a landing as possible.

Because the war had just ended, there were no radio aids to navigation and no radar. All Ray could do was fly by compass and grope his way down upon reaching his destination.

He made a perfect three-point landing and, after he taxied to a makeshift ramp, several trucks immediately appeared and hastily unloaded the precious cargo. What was it? A load of whiskey for the New Year's Eve party for our men so far from home.

Raymond Koehler passed away on July 21, 1994, survived by his widow, Jean, three children and six grandchildren. He had served his country well, and true to form, "remembered Pearl Harbor."

A Beginning and The End

The dropping of the two atomic bombs, conservatively estimated to have saved 1 million American lives, and untold Japanese casualties, was the subject of some revisionism by the Smithsonian Institution. The October 25, 1994, issue of the *Wall Street Journal* referred to the policy as "the transformation of its museums (mostly government-funded) into vehicles for political re-education."

On December 7, 1941, the Japanese Imperial Navy unleashed its unprovoked attack on Pearl Harbor, sinking 18 ships, destroying 174 planes, and killing or wounding 3,681 people. In his declaration of war, President Fanklin D. Roosevelt referred to the day as "a date which will live in infamy."

In quick order, Japanese forces captured the East Indies, Singapore, Guam, Wake Island and Hong Kong. Several months later, the Bataan Peninsula and Corregidor fell.

Maj. David Nemerow, a Brighton, New York, resident who served with the U.S. Army Air Corp's 509th Bomb Group during World War II noted, "In the Air and Space Museum of the Smithsonian Institution, which is preparing an exhibit of the Enola Gay, the B-29 bomber which dropped the atomic bombs,the Japanese are portrayed as defending their homeland against the Americans, with little reference to Japanese aggression that led the way in the first place."

Deep in the recesses of the National Archives in Washington, DC hidden for four decades, within thousands of pages of yellowed, dusty documents was a comprehensive report by the Defense Department — "The Story of the Invasion of Japan." The report detailed what terrible tragedies were in store for us if the invasion had proceeded on November 1, 1945 — the magnitude of Japanese defense plans, and the surprise details of the "divine wind,"better known as the "Kamikaze."

A postscript to the Defense Department document contained a story about an attempted invasion of Japan in the year 1281 by a Chinese fleet of 3,500 ships with 100,000 troops and 900 Korean boats with another 42,000 warriors.

The invasion forces fought a fierce battle with the ill-equipped Japanese defenders, with heavy casualties on both sides. The Koreans were forced to retreat.

During the summer, the Chinese and Korean fleets joined forces and planned another attack. But the Japanese performed ceremonies at all their shrines, praying for divine intervention.

As if in answer to their prayers, a savage typhoon sprang up, struck the invasion fleet with full fury and wreaked havoc upon the ships and the men aboard. The fleet was lost, and casualties exceeded 100,000 soldiers.

The Japanese fervently believed that this "divine wind" would forever protect them.

By July 1945, the Japanese knew that the Americans were planning an invasion. At the same time, they believed that their "divine wind" once again would save them.

A partial list of Japanese defenses included 12,725 Army and Navy planes (4,825 marked as "suicide" planes); a rocket-powered bomb, much like Germany's V-1 but flown by a suicide pilot; 300 suicide submarines; 4,000 motorboats armed with high explosive warheads; magnetic mines around the beaches; 790,000 defenders against an estimated 500,000 U.S. troops; and 29 million Japanese "national volunteer" combat forces, armed with rifles, swords, axes and bamboo spears.

The estimated casualties during the early stages of the invasion would be 1,000 Japanese and American soldiers every hour. Adm. William Leahy estimated that there would be more than 250,000 Americans killed or wounded on Kyushu Island alone. Gen. Charles Willoughby, MacArthur's chief of intelligence, estimated that American casualties from the entire operation would be 1 million soldiers by the fall of 1946. Some staffers considered this a conservative estimate.

Had the two bombs not been dropped and had the war continued, the United States would have been in the process of building an invasion fleet of 180 lightly armed transports, 70 cargo vessels, plus 4,000 aircraft on Okinawa. In September and October, we would have built up our invasion force to 550,000 men in preparation for the November 1 invasion.

As it turned out, on October 8, a gigantic typhoon hit the staging areas, and by the afternoon eventually rose to 150 mph. "Tent City," which had been housing 150,000 U.S. troops ceased to exist.

U.S. Navy Lt. Commander Alva Redfield, a resident of Penfield, wrote the following concerning the two typhoons:

"After the peace treaty was signed, the politicians raised the hue

and cry of 'bring the boys home.' Thus, in September was born Operation Magic Carpet, a plan to use escort carriers and other ships to return all servicemen who had been slated for the invasion of the Japanese home islands. The Makin Island received this new assignment. On the night of September 17, 1945, we rode out a lusty typhoon in Waka-No-Ura Wan harbor. The anemometer blew away at 84 knots (96 mph), which is no breeze. Our planes

Lt. Commander Alva Redfield

were securely lashed below deck. The only casualty was a sailor struck in the head by an oil drum. The carrier took the maximum roll of 37-$\frac{1}{2}$ degrees to starboard and still was able to recover in that wild sea. One degree more, and it would have capsized.

"In October, our squadron spent several days searching for a Mariner seaplane that had gone down with all hands. The search ended when a typhoon ["Kamikaze"] developed in the area and it became too dangerous to fly. Mine was the last plane to land on the pitching, heaving deck with winds of 50 knots blowing over it. The ship barely maintained steerage way. I landed without catching a wire or rolling forward. We evaded the worst of the typhoon, but it devastated Okinawa."

Samuel Eliot Morison, the famous Naval historian, referred to Typhoon Louise as the most furious ever encountered by the U.S.

Navy. Almost 270 ships were sunk, grounded or damaged beyond repair. Fifty-three others were damaged too badly to restore to duty, and out of 90 ships which required major repair, 80 were scrapped. Hundreds of Americans were killed.

In the aftermath, with the war now history, few people concerned themselves with the obsolete invasion plans of Japan. The Japanese prayers for divine intervention were apparently answered. Fortunately for all concerned, it was a month too late.

Closer to home, the sun has yet to set on the "day of infamy." Lying in 65 feet of water, probably within a mile of shore, is the wreckage

This B-24 plane crashed in Lake Ontario in 1944. Paul Roxin was communications officer on duty in Rochester when the tragedy happened.

of a B-24, nicknamed "Getaway Gertie," which crashed into Lake Ontario east of Oswego in 1944. Several months later, the wing washed up on shore and, in 1970, divers came across the wreckage.

Because the crew members still may be entombed there, the Geriatric Pilots Association has given Congresswoman Louise Slaughter all the pertinent details, which have been forwarded to the appropriate government agencies. We hope, a thorough search by a Navy minesweeper eventually will be conducted.

Naughty! Naughty!

Lt. Robert Ferris, USMC

USMC Lt. Robert Ferris explained, "My TBM engine was disabled while strafing enemy positions on Okinawa. I landed in the water and ended up on shore in American-held territory. The tail and the engine had broken off and the wings were sheared off by steel beams that the Japanese had driven into the ground to repel landing craft. My report did not include that I had been over enemy lines, as I was flight-testing a new engine. Regulations stated that test flights were to be conducted within gliding distance of the airstrip. Obviously, to be shot down on a test flight was not in compliance."

"Modest to a fault," may be an accurate way of describing the University of Rochester graduate, Marine Corps pilot. Lt. Robert Ferris.

Two months after walking away from his aborted test flight, he was given an extremely dangerous assignment on Okinawa. With the Japanese holding one-half of the island, a Marine contingent was pinned down in a valley with the Japanese controlling the hills on both sides. The only approach was closed because of torrential rains, preventing trucks from bringing in much needed medical supplies, food, etc.

Weather was definitely a problem at Bob's base, a 400-ft. ceiling and one mile visibility. Because of some problem, when Bob made two passes to the beleaguered Marines, the bomb bay doors failed to open. However, on the third approach, after encountering Japanese mortor shells from both sides of the mountain, he was able to drop the supplies and head back to his base.

One major problem – the weather had deteriorated to a 100-ft. ceiling and one-quarter mile visibility. When queried by the controller whether he wanted to go over the ocean and bail out and they would attempt to fish him out, Bob responded: "Do you know any other funny stories?" and rejected the option.

As it happened, the Marine Corps had just received its GCA (Ground Controlled Approach) equipment, whereby, with radar, the controllers could guide the plane down safely. Bob indicated that he would accept that offer provided the controllers could uncrate the equipment (of course it could not be calibrated nor flight checked).

Within a few minutes, the euipment was assembled and an experienced controller began talking him down. The last part of a controlled approach is a 5-second period of silence and, if all went well, the strip should be dead ahead, and that's precisely what occurred. After 5 seconds, Bob was at the end of the strip and touched down. A miracle in the making.

For his heroism and coolness, and for saving the lives of a number of fellow Marines, Bob was awarded the Distinguished Flying Cross (DFC). Thanks, Bob! All is forgiven!

World War II Pilot Shares His Memories

Lt. John C. Kittrell

By the time World War II ended, P-47 Air Force pilot Lt. John C. Kittrell had completed 100 missions, bombed Hitler's retreat at Berchtesgaden, and was awarded both the Distinguished Flying Cross with one oak leaf cluster and the Air Medal with three oak leaf clusters. Unfortunately, he was brought down by enemy flak and captured by Nazi soldiers, but he then took part in a daring midnight escape.

Kittrell. who was raised in Rochester, graduated from Monroe High School and enlisted in the Army Air Corps in 1942. He joined the 79th Fighters Group, 12th Air Force on the Isle of Corsica and immediately started tactical close-support work for the American 5th Army. This close-support work involved dive-bombing railroad and motor transport bridges, railroad marshaling yards, trains, enemy for-tifications, and fuel dumps, and destroying enemy planes on their own airdromes.

After participating in the southern France invasion and flying from three different air fields in southern France, Kittrell and his organiza-tion flew to the eastern coast of Italy to support the British 8th Army.

On February 20, 1945, Kittrell's was one of eight Thunderbolts that took off for a routine rocket and strafing mission in northern Italy. After determining that their primary area was hidden by a total over-cast in the Alps, they kept on course until noticing a troop train through a hole in the clouds. They strafed the train, and the woods were set on fire.

During interrogation back at the base, it was determined that Kittrell and his group had dropped in at Hitler's retreat in Berchtesgaden. The incident was reported in many papers around the world, including the *New York Times*.

Kittrell's childhood friend and neighbor, B-24 pilot Charles Kenning, who was stationed in London at the time, learned firsthand of his friend's heroics in the *London Daily Mirror*.

Taking on his 100th mission on April 17, 1945, little did Kittrell know it would be his last.

His plane crashed, and he was captured by the Germans. While he and they walked north to a POW camp, the Germans picked up seven more prisoners. A few nights later, at about 4 a.m., Kittrell and his fellow prisoners were led to a house and told by the guards to knock on the door. The guards went out the front gate, leaving the group alone. Kittrell and two others went to the wall in the rear of the yard, climbed over, separated and ran.

Kittrell found British troops who took him back to his air field. He was all through flying in the ETO, however. Once a prisoner, you cannot fly in the same theater again because if you are recaptured you can be shot as a spy.

Lt. Kittrell, who attended Rochester Institute of Technology, was a great American, willing to make the supreme sacrifice so that we would not live under tyranny. He passed away on April 17, 2001, and is greatly missed by his family, friends and fellow members of the Geriatric Pilots Association.

D-Day Memories: The Beginning of the End of World War II

When Dori Gollon of Brighton came downstairs for breakfast on June 6, 1944, she found her mother sitting next to the radio, tears streaming down her cheeks and barely able to speak. In halting words, her mother explained that the long-awaited invasion of Europe had begun: "This is D-Day."

Gen. Dwight Eisenhower had assembled the largest armada in the world's history, as thousands of soldiers, marines and sailors stormed the beachheads of Normandy.

Every church, temple and other house of worship flung open its doors so the nation could pray for the safety of loved ones and for victory.

On the anniversary of D-Day, these courageous and honorable men and women should be saluted and remembered for their heroic contributions to the free world.

"An army marches on its stomach," an adage attributed to Napoleon, was just as true on D-Day as 132 years earlier. On this date, the late Staff Sgt. Louis "Bardy" Bardenstein, who was in charge of mess for officers and enlisted men of the 69th Signal Battalion of the U.S. 3rd Army, stormed Utah Beach. When the beachhead was secured, Bardy moved with his HQ Company in many campaigns and battles, such as Ardennes, Central Europe, Northern France and the Rhineland.

In one town in Germany, his unit came upon an ice cream shop that had been abandoned in the wake of the U.S. Army's approach. Milk and eggs were plentiful at the shop, so they took the equipment and started manufacturing ice cream during the war, serving it at mess halls and sending it in insulated cases to infantry units. For this masterly maneuver, Bardenstein was awarded a bronze star for improving the morale of the soldiers.

On another occasion, while he and some officers were bivouacked in a captured German officer's home, they heard some strange noises at night. What they found was a young Jewish girl who had been hidden in a small room below the stairs, and because her benefactor was no longer there, she was coming out at night searching for food.

By 1952, Capt. Art Devlin of Lake Placid, had won numorous gold medals for the United States ski jumping team.

Capt. Art Devlin, 1952

However, eight years earlier, when he was a B-24 pilot on his 24th mission with the 727th squadron of the 15th Air Force based in Italy, his plane was shot down by anti-aircraft fire and all crew members parachuted to safety.

Later, on D-Day, Devlin and his crew departed Italy, joined with other bomber squadrons from England, dropped their bombs and returned to their base. All in all, he flew 50 missions and spent four years in the Air Force.

Many of us have been accustomed to watching Devlin in the Gillette razor commercials over the course of the years. However, when he won the Gold Medal, and millions of Americans watched with lumps in their throats as the American flag was raised, few knew he won that medal with shrapnel imbedded in his left knee cap from air combat injuries.

He exemplified the finest in loyalty, sacrifice and full commitment to the preservation of freedom.

On D-Day, Lt. Hank Lapinski was still undergoing Operation Crew Training at Ardmore Air Force Base in Oklahoma. Upon completing this

Lt. Hank Lapinski

assignment, he received orders to proceed with his crew to the B-17 manufacturing plant at Lincoln, Nebraska, to transport a new B-17 to the European Theater of Operations.

Said Lapinski:

"The night before leaving Lincoln, I wrote a letter to my wife, Betty, and our 11-month-old daughter, Carol Ann. Knowing our flight took us over Rochester, my plan was to fly low over my in-laws' house and deliver the letter to my wife and daughter by parachute. Because it was almost mid-December, I made a waterproof package with a parachute made out of a pillow case.

"As fate would have it, one of the biggest snowstorms in Rochester history was in progress. Needless to say, instrument flight conditions prevented finding a low fly over.

"As we were using the Rochester radio range for navigation, I instructed the radio operator to drop the chute out the camera well when we hit the cone of silence. The ROC radio range was located on East Henrietta Road near the Erie Canal.

"Needless to say, it never turned up. After arriving in England, I was assigned to the 325th Squadron of the Eighth Air Force and flew 32 missions over enemy territory until the war in Europe ended."

Undoubtedly, historians will note D-Day as the beginning of the end for Adolf Hitler and his Third Reich. World War II had begun with Germany's invasion of Poland on September 1, 1939, a war estimated to have caused the loss of 40 million to 50 million lives.

Charles B. Kenning as
AVIATION CADET US ARMY AIR CORPS
Retired with Rank, Lt. Col. USAAF

American prisoners of war rush out of Hohemark hospital 10 miles from Frankfurt to welcome their rescuers from the Third Army. Arrow indicates 2nd Lt. Charles Kenning.

World War II Pilot and
Former Enemies Reunite

Several years ago, Second Lt. Charles B. Kenning, a former member of the 445th Bomb Group, visited the men who shot down his colleagues over Germany back in September 1944. During this more recent visit to the German town of Bad Hersfeld, he helped dedicate a monument to the 118 Americans and 18 Germans killed when 35 heavy U.S. bombers strayed into the gunsights of 150 Luftwaffe fighters.

The Americans had been part of a huge aerial armada bearing down on the industrial city of Kassel. But a navigation mistake separated them from the main group and its fighter escort and set up one of the worst of day air losses in American Air Force history.

Against that backdrop of carnage, Kenning, then a 20-year-old Army Air Force pilot, reported for combat duty. Kenning became a Rochester lawyer whose offices, from 1953 until recently, were in the Times Square Building.

He often talked about his experiences in the war. The history, events and the people interested him. But he feels his war stories are like those of hundreds of thousands of others – And hundreds of thousands more who didn't live to tell their war stories.

Kenning was a student at St. Bonaventure University when Pearl Harbor was attacked. He and virtually all the men in his class eventually joined the military. On February 22, 1943, he and some 250 other local men left Rochester by train for basic training in Atlantic City. The New Yorkers were put up at the Chalfonte Hotel while they learned to be soldiers.

Through a screening process and months of exhaustive training, Kenning became a B-24 Liberator pilot. He flew at a gunnery school and, early in September 1944, set sail for Britain aboard the Ile de France, a converted luxury liner that hauled 10,000 soldiers, zigzagging through the Atlantic to avoid U-boats.

The 445th (pronounced "4-45th") had come to Europe earlier in the war as part of the U.S. 8th Air Force. In its first months, the group was led by a famous personality, Jimmy Stewart, an officer in the Army Air Corp. The failed Kassel mission gutted the 445th, with just four of its 35 Liberators returning to base.

Jimmy Stewart, 1978

Kenning came in with the replacements to restaff the group and continue its bombing runs over Germany. The flights often took 8 to 12 hours, and the struggle to control the lumbering four-engine planes was physically taxing for the pilots.

On his second mission, Kenning's plane took part in the saturation bombing of Cologne. The city was leveled except for its stunning cathedral, which was just a mile from Kenning's target.

By spring 1945, Kenning's crew was making regular attacks on Magdeburg on the Elbe River. The plane took anti-aircraft fire and was damaged on its first five flights over the city but managed to return safely to base despite extensive damage.

It never returned from the sixth flight, the crew's 24th combat mission. Kenning's plane was the lower left element of the lead squadron in the 445th's March 3 raid on Madgeburg, meaning the first plane in the attack formation was ahead and to the right of the Liberator's cockpit.

The formation began taking fire from anti-aircraft cannons. As flak hit the plane and tore into its fuselage, it reminded Kenning of rocks hitting a tin shed. He could hear it above the roar of the engines. It was truly frightening.

The Americans also came under attack from more than 50 Messerschmitt 262s, new twin-engine turbojet fighters whose speed allowed them to move at will through the pack of lumbering bombers.

In an instant, so quickly there was time only to act on reflex, Kenning saw the tail of the lead plane blown off. The bomber arched up and over and thundered out of control above Kenning's Liberator.

Kenning dove to the right to avoid a collision, knowing his plane was being hit by enemy fire. In a moment he was saturated with 110 octane gasoline. Two engines were out. One was on fire. Part of his left wing had been shot off.

Looking back, Kenning is amazed the plane didn't explode. He calls it a miracle.

The decision was made to bail out, and the crew went out the open bomb bay, into the frigid air at 24,000 feet. It was their first parachute jump. One man's face was frostbitten on the way down. Kenning estimates he free–fell for 10,000 feet and then hung oscillating from his parachute for 20 minutes.

All around him, Kenning saw burning planes and opening parachutes. Then a church steeple swooped upward and past, and he was thrown down onto a railroad bed and pitched headfirst into the ditch beyond it, his right ankle shattered.

The first people to reach him wanted to lynch him. But two German soldiers came, boys 14 and 16 in uniforms and carrying guns. They fortunately saw fit to protect him and took him to solitary confinement.

At home, Kenning's family received a telegram from the War Department. Shot down over enemy territory, missing in action. Weeks passed.

And then Kenning's aunt leafed through the latest copy of *Life* magazine — the April 16, 1945 issue with a head-and-shoulders cover photo of Gen. Dwight D. Eisenhower. Inside, she found gaunt, frightening pictures of newly liberated American prisoners of war.

And on page 27, standing in a crowd of young men on crutches outside a German hospital, was a smiling Second Lt. Charles B. Kenning. It was his family's first word that he had survived.

Kenning later received an Air Medal with oak leaf clusters, and the Purple Heart.

Jimmy Stewart, far left, is among the pilots posing in front of their B-24 Liberator. This crew took part in the bombing of Germany and was eventually shot down.

CPT?
The WTS and
John Paul Vann

Lt. John Paul Vann and Mary June Allen on their wedding day, October 6, 1945.

In 1940, the federal government decided to encourage the growth of aviation by forming the Civilian Pilot Training Program (CPT). Rochester had four active flying schools at the time, and all of these participated in the newly created program.

In January of 1943, RBI teamed up with Hylan Flying Service, Page Airways, Rochester Aeronautical Corp., and Holderman Flying Service to secure a large Air Force contract.

The CPT eventually evolved into a program known as the 51st College Training Detachment, which operated for 16 months and provided thousands of enlisted men with ground school training and 10 hours of actual flight experience.

Sometime that fall, I was at the Palace Theater on North Clinton Avenue for a film featuring B-17 bombers in Europe. And before the movie began, the curtain opened on 300 of our cadets standing ramrod straight and singing the Army Air Corps anthem: "Off we go, into the wild blue yonder..."

It was a very emotional time. Everyone knew someone who was overseas; so this patriotic display caused quite an outburst of emotion.

Among those cadets were several students I had personally trained, including a young man from North Carolina named John Paul Vann, who had come to participate in the War Training Service (WTS) program in September.

Appointed a cadet officer, Vann was responsible for taking attendance and keeping the other cadets in line during classes.

We had only 30 days to get to know the cadets. After that, a new group of 100 was sent in, and we had a whole new list of names and faces to learn. One of the reasons I remember Vann was the two *n's* in his name.

Vann had another connection to Rochester. A few days before Christmas that year, he met a Rochester girl, Mary Jane Allen, at Critic's ice cream parlor on Clinton Avenue just north of Main Street. He shared Christmas Eve dinner at the Allen home but was shipped out to Tennessee Christmas Day with the rest of his class.

Vann's military career and service in Vietnam later became the subject of the acclaimed and controversial 1988 book, *A Bright Shining Lie: John Paul Vann and America in Vietnam*, by Neil Sheehan, a Vietnam war correspondent for United Press International and *The New York Times*.

In his book (adapted into a 1998 HBO film starring Bill Paxton), Sheehan reported that Vann, who pursued a career in the military after his stint in Rochester, believed we could win the war if we confronted the Communist Vietcong using their own tactics.

Much like his friend, Brig. Gen. Edward Lansdale, an unassuming but perceptive cold warrior (immortalized in the novel *The Ugly American*) critical of our conduct of the war, Vann tried to voice his opinions to the U.S. General in Saigon and his staff in 1963 before the Southeast Asian country drew the U.S. into what became a tragic quagmire. But his views were disregarded as unrealistic. He was reassigned to the Pentagon, and he opted to retire in July of that year.

But Vann returned to Vietnam as a civilian representative for the Agency for International Development (AID), which in those days was often used to front CIA operations. And despite his maverick notions, by May of 1971 he was the senior advisor for the Central Highlands region, with authority over all U.S. military troops in the area.

Though officially a civilian employed by AID, Vann was actually a U.S. Army major general, with joint command of 158,000 South Vietnamese troops, a fact that made him the most important person in the country besides the U.S. ambassador and the commanding general in Saigon.

Vann's influence arguably might have helped lead the Vietnam War toward some sort of uneasy détente (as in Korea) or, in the alternative, hastened our decision to withdraw from South Vietnam (as we did in 1975). But only a week before a scheduled return to the States in 1971, he was killed in a helicopter crash.

Stanley Steinberg, a former Brighton resident who was in Vann's class here recalled: "We were here together at RBI in 1943 and we both shipped out Christmas Day to Nashville. At that point we were separated into different areas for specific training: pilot, navigation, and so on.

"That was the last time I saw him. After he died, I saw the article in the paper and dug out my photo album. I had a picture of him that I thought his wife would like," he said.

And Vann's wife turned out to be none other than the girl from Critic's ice cream shop whom he'd met before shipping out for Tennessee.

Sheehan wrote that Vann and Allen continued their romance through the mail and were married in Rochester two years after they met.

The Bomb: Best Answer for the Time

The horrors and devastating effects of the nuclear age came upon us on August 6, 1945, when America dropped the first atomic bomb on the industrial port city of Hiroshima, Japan, followed just three days later by another bomb on Nagasaki.

These appalling new weapons of mass destruction not only wreaked untold havoc and caused an estimated 100,000 deaths and some 110,000 serious injuries, but they ushered in the Cold War, which occupied the world's attention for decades to follow.

It has been hotly debated ever since whether President Truman's decision to employ such a weapon was correct. While many who didn't live during those dreadful war years found it easy to deplore the government's decision to bring Japan to its knees by such drastic means, dropping the bomb was the only recourse in the minds of others, especially those who had the misfortune to experience the horrific effects of war first hand.

These people included many Rochesterians, like Kenneth Engel, who attended Franklin High School. He was unlucky enough to be captured by the Japanese during the fall of Corregidor in May 1942, becoming one of the 2,300 American prisoners out of nearly 10,000 who died as a result of the infamous Bataan Death March.

And Marine Corps pilot Sam Atlas was a member of a Lockheed Ventura night bombing squadron nearly decimated in engagements at Guadalcanal in the Solomon Islands.

Dorothy Beavers was a teenager then and didn't experience combat but remembers the agonizing times.

"I was too young to join the Women's Army Corps, but I did join the Civil Air Patrol as an aircraft spotter," she said. Noting how relentless the Japanese forces were in the early years of World War II when they invaded China, Korea, Burma and Indonesia, she compared the Japanese to the Nazis in Europe, noting: "History rarely mentions the Japanese in the same terrible light as the Nazis."

After the war ended in 1945, she met and married her husband,

Leo, who had fought on the rugged volcanic island of Iwo Jima. He was only 20 then and still had nightmarish recollections of the experience.

"Because the Japanese were such fearless and determined fighters, they wouldn't give up, and nearly half of my buddies were killed in front of me," he told her.

Beavers is among those convinced that dropping the bomb was the only thing to do.

"My husband's division was getting ready to invade the Japanese mainland when the Hiroshima bomb was dropped. That made an invasion of Japan unnecessary and saved many lives on both sides."

She admitted the destruction and loss of life was "awful," but, like others who have viewed the now-declassified War Department documents, she believed even more destruction would have ensued had the U.S. invaded — Japan had also been working on a similar weapon of mass destruction and would have used it if we hadn't beaten them to the punch.

Beavers lamented the toll that war takes in terms of human suffering.

"War is indeed terrible," she said, "whether it was World War II or

Floyd S. Adams

Vietnam, Bosnia, Grenada, or Haiti." She fears that man still hasn't learned that war isn't a long-term solution to problems, but that sometimes extraordinary means are necessary to halt a conflict that just won't end, as in 1945.

The Geriatric Pilots Association often has met with high school students and various groups, recounting flying experiences and adventures and educating audiences with little appreciation for what happened 50 years ago in Europe and the Pacific.

Our credo is that we not only preserved our freedom and way of life but also helped rebuild Japan and Europe in a spirit of cooperation and forgiveness.

Staff Sargeant Floyd Adams, formerly of Bergen, New York (and a 1949 Eastman School of Music graduate), landed in Japan shortly after hostilities ceased. He observed deep trenches and enormous fortifications with sand bags to be used to protect the country.

He commented, "Had it been necessary to invade, the total casualties, ours and theirs, would have been staggering. Germany, Russia, Italy, Japan and the United States were simultaneously working on the bomb. If any one of our enemies had completed it first, they would certainly have used it on us. As long as it had been made, it had to be tested in a real world context to deter any further use of it."

Bill Pearce "Home Again"

The best news we ever received, afer almost two years in the Pacific, was on August 7, 1945. It was the day after the Enola Gay

William Pearce. Bill was president of WXXI, Rochester's FM classical music station from 1969-1996. (War time picture, Bill was a Signal Man for the US Navy, Beach Invasions).

dropped the bomb. We were enroute to the Marianas, Tinian and Ulithi, to get resupplied before our next landing on Japan's southern island, Kyushu. Those of us in the Fifth Amphibious Force attached to the USS Windsor had been through nine invasions, Kwajalein to Okinawa, seven on D-Day. Each one met with stiffer enemy resistance. As we got closer to Japan casualties increased with each landing. By the time we reached Okinawa the Kamikaze attacks became daily, sometimes hourly. We did not look forward to trying to occupy the Japanese homeland. We knew that would be the last landing for many of us, so we had nothing but praise for Paul Tibbits and his crew. There is no doubt in my mind that thousands of us are alive today because of that single bombing raid on August 6, 1945. As it turned out our amphibious group put the first army occupation forces ashore at a peaceful Yokohama just a few days after the Japanese surrender.

Enola Gay

Pictured above: USN Commander (USNR) Samuel A. Cooper Jr. (center) with USAF (Retired) Brigadier General Paul W. Tibbets (right), pilot of the Enola Gay which dropped the atomic bomb on Hiroshima on August 6, 1945. Person on left not identified. Photograph by Richard E. Bragg.

Ray Moulton became a captain with Mohawk Airlines; Mike Locania became director of maintenance for American Airlines in Los Angeles; and Clarence Robinson (along with Senator Pritchard Strong) were killed in a plane crash in Albany in 1937.

On August 29, 1933, Wiley Post became the first man to circle the globe alone.

Taylor Cub Co. owners Gilbert and Gordon Taylor. Gordon died in an air crash over Detroit in 1929.

Mr. Schwikert and Mae Jenkins in the early 1930s. This was one of the first aircraft built by Taylor Bros. in Rochester.

Celebrity Encounters

A local photographer captured Charles Lindbergh's 1927 landing at Rochester's airport.

When Lindbergh Came to Rochester

For months in 1927, the media publicized the efforts of various intrepid aviators to be the first to accomplish a solo nonstop flight from New York to Paris, thereby claiming the $25,000 prize offered by hotel owner Raymond Orteig.

In May, Charles A. Lindbergh, a former airmail pilot, set a coast-to-coast record, flying from San Diego to Long Island in 21 hours and 20 minutes. The success of this flight piqued the public's interest in aviation.

Then on May 20, he departed Roosevelt Field at 7:52 am, and arrived at LeBourget Field near Paris 33 hours later, receiving a wild, tumultuous greeting from 100,000 people and electrifying the world with his feat.

No single event, not even the initial flight of the Wright Brothers, had captured the hearts and adulation of the hero-worshiping public like the success of Lindbergh's epic adventure.

When word arrived that Lindbergh would visit Washington following a ticker-tape parade in New York City, Arthur Crapsey Sr., a *Times-Union* reporter, arranged to fly to Washington in a Pitcairn biplane flown by Gareth Clark to invite the famous aviator to visit Rochester. Congressman Meyer Jacobstein, who represented this area, assisted in making preparations.

On July 29, Lindbergh visited Rochester and was presented a pen and pencil set and a scroll on behalf of the citizens of the community.

A few hours earlier, the city of Syracuse had presented Lindbergh with a 140-piece set of Syracuse china.

What was life like in Rochester in 1927, and what were the people discussing in those days?

That year, Babe Ruth hit 60 home runs. Many citizens followed the trial of professed anarchists Sacco and Vanzetti, who were convicted and executed (most likely wrongfully) allegedly for slaying a paymaster and a guard.

Local theaters were showing *Ben Hur*, starring Ramon Navarro, Francis X. Bushman, and May McAvoy.

Rochester schoolchildren were enjoying the benevolence of George Eastman's contribution to the school system: Any students who wanted to play a musical instrument merely needed to secure a note from their orchestra director, and they were supplied a free instrument and free music lessons.

The following personal observations demonstrate how Lindbergh's epic flight influenced many to a career in aviation.

Joe Clemow, retired chief pilot, Eastman Kodak Company

Joe Clemow, a Brighton resident who served for many years as chief pilot for Eastman Kodak Co., said, "When I was quite young, my brother, my cousin, and I managed to save the $5 necessary to buy a very short flight in a World War I Jenny plane from a hayfield near town. Later, Lindbergh worked in my hometown, Billings, Montana, as an automobile mechanic prior to his flight across the Atlantic. I was among the crowd at Lambert Field, St. Louis, Missouri, in June when Lindbergh returned with the Spirit of St. Louis. It was a thrill to be there and to see him."

And that fall, Lindbergh flew to 82 cities, including all 48 state capitals. Thus, he landed at Helena, Montana, not Billings. However, his estimated time to fly over was known, and Clemow and his entire grade school went outdoors to see him circle their city.

"Everyone was suddenly interested in Lindbergh and aviation," Clemow said.

Thirteen years later, the Civil Pilot Training (CPT) program and the Army Air Corps started Clemow on a flying career.

"I never met or saw Charles Lindbergh," T. Cyril Noon of Pittsford said, "but his flight from New York to Paris had a profound impact on me as a boy of 11. Pictures of Lindbergh and his airplane were everywhere, so I felt like I knew him."

Noon recalled thinking that the *Spirit of St. Louis* was the most beautiful thing made by man. "I built many models of it and many other flying model airplanes."

Airplanes for Noon became a lifelong passion. He attended the University of Iowa and studied aeronautical engineering, and the engineering degree made possible a career in aerospace work.

World War II brought Noon into Army service, where he took flying training and served out the war as an engineering officer and test pilot. In the past half century, he has been privileged to pilot about 100 different kinds of airplanes.

"I am as fascinated with airplanes as ever, and I'm still licensed to fly," Noon said.

David "Scotty" Caplan of Brighton actually remembers the excitement generated when the newspapers reported that Lindbergh would be stopping in Rochester.

"I asked my parents if I could go and see him and also take my younger brother. At the time, I was 15 and Isadore was 7," Caplan recalled. "As I held my brother's hand, we boarded a streetcar at Joseph Avenue, then transferred to another at Main Street, and again at Genesee Street. The line ended at Scottsville Road, and from there, we walked to Britton Road Airport.

"Everybody was scanning the sky to see who would be the first to spot Lindbergh's airplane. It seemed to me we waited at least two hours before a roar went up and the plane suddenly appeared over the airport."

In retrospect, Caplan said, Lindbergh certainly influenced him and his brother because in the coming years, they both became licensed pilots.

Other than the Caplan brothers, among the 50,000 area residents who flocked to Britton Field was a musician who played oboe with the Eastman Theater Orchestra. Gus Konz was so moved by what he witnessed that he decided to shift gears and learned to fly, becoming a commercial pilot in 1929. Among Konz's students was a precocious young oboe player named Mitch Miller.

In 1936, Konz took a position with American Airlines and flew for the company for many years until reaching the mandatory retirement age of 60.

Also looking on in awe and admiration when Lindbergh arrived here was Rochester's youngest licensed pilot, Vic Evans, who was all of 17 years of age. In part, Evans followed in Lindbergh's footsteps by becoming an airmail pilot.

In 1936, Evans also joined American Airlines, opening the door for many Rochesterians to obtain positions with the company.

Several years later, he was flying a DC-3 when the stewardess entered the cockpit and said to him, "You have a celebrity on board."

Vic replied, "Really? Who?" The stewardess calmly answered, "Charles Lindbergh."

That is all Evans had to hear. Immediately recalling seeing him in Rochester on his visit here, Evans invited Lindbergh into the cockpit, and the two had an animated chat.

"Wow," Evans would brag to his grandchildren, "I took Lindbergh for an airplane ride!"

Don Zimmer Was Married on My Call

Manager Don Zimmer says the best time of his life was when the Cubs won the NL East title in 1984.

Residents of the Southern Tier may recall that the summer of 1951 was far from the driest on record. So it wasn't unusual that rain was falling when the author reported for duty one afternoon in late August at Chemung County Airport, in Elmira, New York.

Upon entering the operations office of the Civil Aeronautics Administration (CAA), I was greeted by the usual clatter of Teletype machines spewing forth terminal and airway forecasts, hourly weather reports and flight plans. Airway traffic control clearances were being transmitted on telephone networks, and pilots were reporting their positions to various ground stations — all par for the course.

The first words uttered by Ronnie Ogden, whose watch I was relieving, were, "Buster, you're going to be playing Cupid this evening."

"What's that supposed to mean?" I asked.

Ogden replied: "You know, Don Zimmer, our ever-popular short-stop of the Elmira Pioneers, and his fiancée are due to be married at the stadium tonight at 7, with the regular ballgame to follow the ceremony.

"Also, you are undoubtedly aware that fans have been collecting funds for months to buy the couple a new car as a wedding gift.

"And you know what miserable weather we've been having all day. So, at five minutes to 6 you're going to get a call from the local radio station. And it will be your call whether or not to postpone the wedding and the game, or to proceed according to plan. How does that grab you?"

My initial reaction was: "Gosh, my own marriage to Beatrice Caro in Utica is only three weeks away. And here this pretty young bride-to-be isn't even sure a wedding will take place in three hours."

Dazed but undaunted, I spent the next hour and 55 minutes watching the sky, examining weather forecasts, and contacting every plane coming down the pike, which included American Airlines, United, Mohawk, and even Joe Clemow and co-pilot Herb Schultz in Kodak's DC-3, NC65601 (I still remember the aircraft identification!).

Sure enough, at 5:55 pm the phone rang. The caller identified himself as the radio station announcer and asked apprehensively, "What's the verdict?"

"Go for broke!" I replied. And the weather held.

The following day, local papers carried a vivid description of the wedding. Both teams formed an arch of crossed bats from the dugout to home plate. Our hero was in uniform, with his bride wearing the traditional long white gown. To add to the gala ceremony, an organ was brought to the stadium and played such favorites as "I Love You Truly."

As thousands of fans looked on, many of them misty eyed and others with tears streaming down their cheeks, the wedding nuptials were completed. However, our shortstop, although he came up to bat three times, never reached first base once.

"It was a beautiful wedding at home plate," remembered Pittsford resident Brad Phelps, who had just graduated from college and had begun working for American-LeFrance in Elmira.

"My boss was a director of the Pioneers, and I got to know Don Zimmer very well. He was a great guy. It was a beautiful ballpark. The moon would come up over center field. It was lovely," Phelps said.

In 1972, or 21 years later, members of the Rochester Philharmonic Orchestra were preparing for a fund-raising concert for the residents of the Southern Tier, which had been hard hit by a terrible flood as a result of Hurricane Agnes. Bill Givens, the popular radio announcer for WHAM, was the master of ceremonies. Because Elmira was one of the cities especially devastated, I mentioned that I lived there, and Bill noted he also came from Elmira.

One thing led to another, and the matter of the wedding at Pioneer Stadium came up. Bill had been in radio at the time and knew the event well, but it appeared he wasn't the announcer who had phoned me.

Givens passed away a few years later, and his family donated his entire musical collection to St. John Fisher College in Pittsford, New York. Then-president Father Charles Lavery invited my wife and me to the dedication, where we met Jack Slattery, one of my favorite WHAM hosts who had been with the station for decades. When I casually mentioned Bill Givens' knowledge of the Zimmer wedding in Elmira many years earlier, Jack started to laugh.

"What's so funny?" I asked. Jack replied, "Paul, I was the sports announcer for WELM and called all their ballgames, including the description of the entire wedding!" Jack hadn't been the unidentified caller, but I'm convinced it was Bill Givens. If any reader can confirm this or knows it was someone else, I'd welcome a call or letter.

After a lapse of several years, our daughter Wendy called from Boston one evening. It happened that the rent on their apartment was being raised 50 percent, and she and her husband simply couldn't swing it. They made a decision to purchase a home in Reading, Massachusetts, some 12 miles northwest of Boston. So, one blustery weekend in January, my wife Bea and I decided to check it out.

While Bea was in the living room talking with the owner, I was in the kitchen browsing. Suddenly, there was a shriek from the living room. I quickly rushed to see what the problem was. Pointing to a picture of a newly wedded couple, Bea gasped excitedly, "Paul, you simply won't believe this!"

The lady mentioned that the groom was a very close friend of one of their sons, and when this youngster's mother passed away when he was only 14, the father decided to move the family to Florida. Because the boy wanted to remain in the same school, the owners "adopted" him as their own.

At this point, she mentioned that their "son's" bride was the daughter of a well-known Boston sports celebrity. When Bea asked, "And whom might that be?" the lady simply replied, "She's the daughter of Don Zimmer, manager of the Boston Red Sox," at which point the commotion ensued. "My husband called the shots way back in 1951 for their wedding at the baseball stadium in Elmira, New York."

She knew all about the wedding at the ball field, the threatening weather, and the decision to go ahead with the ceremony. In response to my question whether she was in touch with the Zimmers, she replied, "Yes, frequently. We visit them in their winter home in Bradenton, Florida."

To which I piped up, "Tell Don he owes me an autographed baseball, because I happened to be the one who made the decision to proceed with the wedding and ball game."

About two weeks later I received a very warm letter from Mrs. Zimmer. And when Bea and I returned to Reading for a Fourth of July weekend, our daughter said, "Dad, I have something for you." She went upstairs and returned with a small box. I opened it and found a brand new baseball autographed by Don Zimmer and all the members of the Texas Rangers, the team he was then managing.

It's a small world.

In Memoriam

George Cheatham

George Cheatham, Pilot Extraordinaire

When we recall some of the shenanigans that occurred at the Rochester airport during the 1930s, no story would be complete without mentioning the colorful and checkered career of George Cheatham.

A graduate of Edison Tech High School, Cheatham, earned his wings at D.W. Airport in Le Roy. He first appeared on the scene in 1935 as the alternate pilot for the Gannett Newspapers' Stinson Reliants and later as co-pilot for their Stinson tri-motor. Cheatham always was available for other sundry duties, such as ferrying passengers on short area hops (he got the usual 60 cents for two passengers; the salesman, — I got 30).

In August 1937, the Rochester Pilots Association was invited by the Toronto Flying Club to spend the weekend as their guests. In those days, the Toronto Airport was little more than a hay lot with two wooden T-hangers about four miles north of Toronto.

Al Ritz, a fledgling pilot at that time, rented our Waco, and away we went with 30 mph headwinds. When we were unable to locate the field, I took over and decided to land before we ran out of gas.

The field where we landed had a high barbed wire fence around it. As a young boy walked by, I asked where the airport was. "Just two miles west," he replied.

We took off, found the field, and landed. By then Al and I probably resembled a scene from Nelson Eddy and Jeanette McDonald's *Rose Marie*.

The fact that we were running low on fuel and landed was forgivable. The fact that we departed without clearing customs was strictly frowned upon, but still forgivable. But what really irked officials of our friendly neighbors to the north was that our chosen landing "field" was none other than a prison farm.

The authorities were suspicious and asked: "What's an American plane doing on our prison farm?" They nearly impounded it!

That night, after a scrumptious meal, we went to a nightspot called Club Esquire. Most of us ordered Cokes at 10 cents apiece. Then we were told it was "plus a $6 cover charge."

Cheatham, who at that point was feeling pretty happy, picked up an empty Coke bottle and was ready to heave the bottle right at the bar's beautiful blue stained glass mirror. He said to the manager, "I'll tell you what we're going to do. We'll pay 10 cents apiece for the Coke — no $6 cover charge. Otherwise, I'm going to fling this !#$*!? bottle right through your pretty mirror." And he would have.

The owner thought better of it and accepted our offer; we left for Sunnyside Amusement Park, where we again managed to disrupt things, all under the aegis of George Cheatham. For some strange reason, we never were invited to return to Toronto.

As a 1937 promotion for the Christmas season, the Gannett papers had planned a stunt two days before Thanksgiving. Their Stinson Reliant was sprayed with a luminous paint depicting Santa Claus and his eight reindeer (Rudolph had yet to arrive on the scene).

That day, both papers carried a story on how Santa would arrive for a preview about 8 pm Also in the plane was their favorite newscaster, the redoubtable Al Sigl.

Shortly after the plane took off, an old Ben Franklin schoolmate and buddy, Roy Bauer, showed up at the airport and wanted to take a ride over the city. Our flight lasted only about 10 minutes, and when we pulled up on the ramp, several hundred parents and their children surrounded our plane, thinking we had Santa on board. After explaining Santa was on another plane, the crowd anxiously waited for Cheatham and Sigl to land, which they did about 20 minutes later.

But where was Santa Claus?

Apparently, the luminous paint depicting Santa and his reindeer failed to adhere to the fuselage and blew off during the flight. When Cheatham and Sigl surveyed the fuselage, they were heartbroken for the kids waiting for Santa. Cheatham was so furious that all he could do was mutter "Wait 'til I get my hands on that goddamn painter."

The following afternoon, a student wanted to practice some landings, and, as I had something else to do, I asked Cheatham if he would ride with him. Of course, he obliged. He asked me, "How's the gas situation?" I replied, "OK," because it would be only a 15-minute flight.

On the first approach, the Lycoming engine sputtered once and quit — out of gas! Cheatham made an emergency landing in a field just short of the airport itself, and, luckily, there was no damage to the plane.

When I saw him a few minutes later, after our plane was towed in, he was livid with anger. I apologized for my mistake, but my immediate reaction was to think: "Suppose that had happened the night before when I was flying over downtown Rochester? 'What fools ye mortals be.' "

The next year, I went to work for the Civil Aeronautics in administration, and Cheatham went to work for Braniff Airlines. 1937 and 1938, we saw the exodus of many pilots from the Rochester airport, because the airlines were expanding and hiring pilots.

After serving at several different airports for a number of years, I was transferred back to Rochester. One morning in January 1942, I arrived at the airport to find a Braniff DC-3 on the ramp. We were at war then, and unusual things were beginning to happen. About 9 am, up walked Capt. George Cheatham, pilot of the DC-3 to file a flight plan.

My first remark was, "What are you doing here? Braniff is a Texas airline."

Cheatham gave me the details. They had a charter flight for Uncle Sam from Dallas to New York for repatriation of some foreign nationals.

On the return, he'd left LaGuardia for Dallas. "I figured I was somewhere over West Virginia but got lost, and when I broke out of the heavy overcast, I was right over the middle of this damn airport, so I decided to land here and spend the night with my folks!"

That was the last time I saw Cheatham. He went on to become chief pilot (out of 700) for Braniff and retired several years later upon reaching the magic retirement age — 60.

I was truly saddened when I learned this remarkable man had passed away.

How Prophetic - V-mail

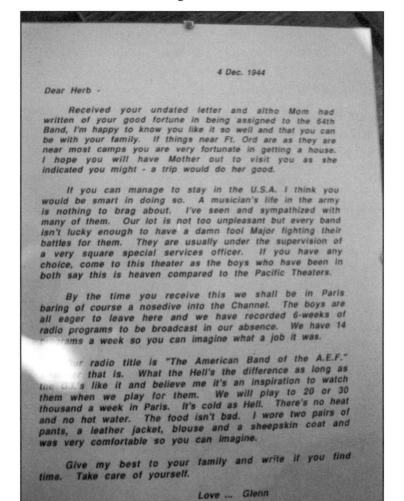

4 Dec. 1944

Dear Herb -

Received your undated letter and altho Mom had written of your good fortune in being assigned to the 64th Band, I'm happy to know you like it so well and that you can be with your family. If things near Ft. Ord are as they are near most camps you are very fortunate in getting a house. I hope you will have Mother out to visit you as she indicated you might - a trip would do her good.

If you can manage to stay in the U.S.A. I think you would be smart in doing so. A musician's life in the army is nothing to brag about. I've seen and sympathized with many of them. Our lot is not too unpleasant but every band isn't lucky enough to have a damn fool Major fighting their battles for them. They are usually under the supervision of a very square special services officer. If you have any choice, come to this theater as the boys who have been in both say this is heaven compared to the Pacific Theaters.

By the time you receive this we shall be in Paris baring of course a nosedive into the Channel. The boys are all eager to leave here and we have recorded 6-weeks of radio programs to be broadcast in our absence. We have 14 ......ams a week so you can imagine what a job it was.

....r radio title is "The American Band of the A.E.F." .... that is. What the Hell's the difference as long as .... s like it and believe me it's an inspiration to watch them when we play for them. We will play to 20 or 30 thousand a week in Paris. It's cold as Hell. There's no heat and no hot water. The food isn't bad. I wore two pairs of pants, a leather jacket, blouse and a sheepskin coat and was very comfortable so you can imagine.

Give my best to your family and write if you find time. Take care of yourself.

Love ... Glenn

Courtesy of Glenn Miller Family

114

Glenn Miller and Irene Manning on Thanksgiving Day, 1944 after a recording session.

Memories of Glenn Miller

On December 15 and 16, 1944, two tragic events occurred in Europe that had a sobering and depressing effect upon the Western world. On December 15, Maj. Glenn Miller departed from an RAF strip in England bound for Paris and was never heard from again.

Ironically, on December 4, in the first sentence of a letter to his

Irene Manning, graduate of Eastman School of Music.

brother, Herb, he remarked: "By the time you receive this, we shall be in Paris barring a nosedive into the Channel." How prophetic!

On December 16, the German army unleashed a vicious counterattack against the Allied forces with some 250,000 men. This battle became known as the Battle of the Bulge and resulted in 81,000 American casualties.

After five weeks of intense fighting, weakened by the loss of 100,000 soldiers, the Nazi army was driven

115

back to where the battle had begun.

Now, more than five decades later, we remain a free and democratic people, and the legacy of Glenn Miller's music is as strong and popular as ever.

In 1937, Miller formed his own band and in 1939 produced a sensational breakthrough with his introduction of three great hits: "In the Mood," "Moonlight Serenade" and "Chattanooga Choo-choo."

Shortly after Japan's attack on Pearl Harbor on December 7, 1941, followed by Germany's declaration of war against the United States, Miller wrote the War Department suggesting he and his band be incorporated into military service.

In due time, a 60-piece band was organized, with players from his civilian band coupled with other musicians. Advanced training was held at Yale University, and on June 28, 1944, after a rough crossing of the Atlantic on the *Queen Elizabeth*, the band arrived in England. Between dodging buzz bombs, the band began a grueling schedule of radio broadcasts, personal appearances at Army and Air Force bases, and recording for the American Broadcasting System in Europe (ABSIE).

On Thanksgiving Day, just a few weeks before Miller's disappearance, Irene Manning, an opera singer who had attended the Eastman School Music (Class of '34) on a four year scholarship (working at McCurdy's for $3 on Saturdays to earn spending money), signed on with Maj. Miller in London.

This turned out to be a banner year for Manning. Having toured with her own USO four-girl unit for months entertaining the 8th Air Force and at various hospitals throughout England, she met with Miller and his band on Thanksgiving to record four American pop songs in Germany for the Office of War Information (OWI) and ABSIE.

Miller and his men were ready when Manning arrived. Though she had only one hour to memorize the German lyrics, her classical education at Eastman proved immensely helpful because she could sing in four languages. Miller's extraordinary musicianship and ability to create unique tonal effects led him to conclude that Manning was not the usual band singer. Her classical background revealed itself in a sensitive interpretation of the lyrics and her musical phrasing.

The session was done at Abbey Road Studios, and included "All the Things You Are," "Mary's A Grand Old Name," "Long Ago and Far Away," and concluded with "Begin the Beguine."

In the 1942 James Cagney movie *Yankee Doodle Dandy*, Irene Manning sang two numbers: "Mary's A Grand Old Name" and "45 Minutes From Broadway."

This was an unusual twist, doing "Begin the Beguine." The orchestration was written in the key of F and couldn't be changed. It was too high to sing as written, so Miller suggested Manning sing it an octave lower. She never had done that before — singing in the "chest," à la Marlene Dietrich. She tried, and it was a huge success. Once again, her professionalism stood out as a testimony to the classical music education she had received.

Although there were other recording sessions with his band featuring soloists like Johnny Desmond, Tex Beneke and Ray McKinley, a glance at the band's schedule (listed in *The Glenn Miller Army Air Force Band* by Edward F. Polic) indicates Manning was the last female guest soloist under Miller's personal direction.

On December 12, Miller received orders to fly to Paris via an Air Transport Command plane. The ATC was organized by C.R. Smith, on leave as president of American Airlines, whose operations closely adhered to scheduled airline procedure. ATC had a large selection of twin and four-engine planes, such as the famous C-47 and C-54, all equipped with proper de-icing equipment.

From the exact written order as it appears in Geoffrey Butcher's book on Miller's wartime band, *Next To A Letter from Home*:

1. You will proceed by military aircraft (ATC) on or about 16 December 1944 from present station to SUPREME HQ AEF MAIN on the Continent to carry out the instruction of the AC of SUPREME HQ AEF, and on completion thereof return to present station.

2. Travel on military aircraft as directed. Baggage allowance is limited to six five (65) pounds.

The original plan was for Miller to depart in one of the three

C-47s designated to carry the band to Paris. However, extremely bad weather had settled over the entire continent, and all ATC flights were canceled. When a Lt. Col. Baesell learned that Miller was anxious to get to Paris to organize the forthcoming concerts, he invited Miller to join him the following day. Throwing all caution to the wind, Miller agreed.

On December 15, the weather improved slightly, and the famous C-64 Norseman, an excellent single-engine transport built in Montreal (but not equipped for handling icing conditions) landed at Twinwood Farm.

When the C-64 landed, the ceiling was estimated at about 200 feet and ground temperature was near freezing. Ironically, Miller told his public relations officer, 2nd Lt. Don Haynes: "Haynsie, even the birds are grounded today."

Without even stopping the engine, pilot John Morgan pulled the plane up to the ramp. Col. Baessell handed up his luggage (which included a case of empty champagne bottles he wanted to exchange for full ones in Paris).

Within a minute of departure, the plane was in the clouds, and one can only surmise that with the temperature dropping roughly three degrees every 1,000 feet of altitude, the aircraft picked up a hefty load of ice on the wings, tail section and perhaps the propeller. We'll probably never know exactly what happened, but in all probability, the ice caused a loss of lift, and the plane crashed in the English Channel.

Maj. Glenn Miller rendered a service to his country that remains unforgettable. As with many soldiers, his dedication to his duty cost him his life, but, fortunately, his music is a legacy treasured by millions of faithful fans throughout the world.

What a shame when one of our local radio stations changed its format from the classic hits of the '40s and '50s to what many music lovers refer to as "plastic music." The music of Miller is seldom heard on the radio these days — "Tommy Long, we miss you."

Gus Konz and Victor Evans in the summer of 1934.

Victor Evans, Pilot for Over 60 Years

Victor "Vic" Evans was a former pilot for Gannett Newspapers and American Airlines who started flying at the old Britton Field (now Greater Rochester International Airport) in 1925 and soloed by the age of 15.

A gregarious person, Victor was a fearless pilot, one of only a dozen in the world to perform an outside loop, using a Kinner "Fleet" from D.W. Airport in Le Roy to perform the dangerous maneuver.

In 1929, he served as chief pilot for Colonial Western Airlines out of Utica, New York, and in the early '30s he was an instructor in Rochester.

After completing an instrument course on the West Coast, he returned to Rochester as co-pilot to Russ Holderman, flying the Gannett Newspaper Stinson Tri-Motor.

In 1936, he was hired by American Airlines (he was the first from the Rochester area) and was assigned to fly with Cy "Shorty" Bittner, the airline's dean and practical jokester.

During this period, business was fair in the summer months, but, because of the lack of public acceptance, it was reduced to a few passengers in the winter.

A few years later, Vic was promoted to full pilot with American. All the airline's DC-3s were part of their flagship fleet. As part of American's promotion, when the plane taxied in after landing, the co-pilot would stick a small AA pennant in a holder just outside the cockpit window and would remove it prior to departure.

On Dec. 24, 1944, Victor and co-pilot Dick Lyons departed Detroit en route to Chicago. He was fortunate to land the DC-3 in a field following a mid-air collision with a Piper Cub near Ypsilanti, Michigan.

Part of DC-3s wing was sheared off and part of the Cub was embedded in the DC-3. Victor landed his partially disabled plane on a snow-covered farm without a scratch to his crew or passengers. After a few seconds, the co-pilot turned to Vic and asked, "What do I do now?" In his typically fearless and inimitable style, Vic barked, "Put out the damn flag!" (which, incidentally, was done).

One of the many commendations he received during his career was for that feat.

Victor was a member of the Quiet Birdman (QB), an honorary flying fraternity, and helped found the Rochester Pilots Association in 1934.

Just Call Me Sandy: A Special Pilot Remembered

Sandy Lindsay III, 1947

Sit back for a moment and count the times in your life when you've chanced to meet that extraordinarily special person who would have a profound effect on you. Maybe five times? Six, perhaps?

Whoever these individuals were — teachers, friends, charismatic public personalities — chances are that their influence was so special that just by knowing them you became a finer person yourself.

When Alexander "Sandy" Lindsay III passed away in the spring of 1964, Rochester mourned the passing of one of its own. A man who had been born into such privileged circumstances that he could easily have not worked a day in his life, he instead chose to live each day as if it were his last, leaving his *joie de vivre*, decency, and courage as an enduring memorial to the people whose lives he touched. They included his loving family, with whom he could never spend enough time.

For those of you who remember, and those of you who can imagine, take yourself back to a time when movies cost a quarter and you could fill your gas tank for less than $1.

The August afternoon was hot and sultry when a flashy Chevy roadster came barreling into the parking lot at the Rochester Airport. The driver was a precocious 16-year-old wearing a helmet with chin straps hanging loose who wanted to spend $1.50 for his first airplane ride.

When he announced he was Alexander Lindsay III, Bob Cansdale, Elmer Page, and I were not unduly impressed, even though none of us could even afford $25 to buy a cheap car. Be that as it may, I sold him a ride.

Guy Stratton was the pilot, and the plane was a Waco F. I collected my usual 15-cent commission, enough to purchase a Coke and hot dog the next day for lunch at Strubles Restaurant at the field.

Almost a year had elapsed when Alexander Lindsay III appeared at the airport again, this time as a student of Ray Hylan, and he quietly let it be known that he preferred to be called by his nickname, "Sandy."

When he came for his lessons, Sandy usually was accompanied by three or four young ladies who attended either the Harley School or the Columbia school and were always stunning in their neat and expensive clothes. One, however, stood out above the rest. She was Jean Sampson, whose father was a physician with offices on Culver Road, and there was no denying that she and Sandy were made for each other.

One day not too long after he began taking lessons, while I taxied out with a student and awaited our turn for takeoff, I noticed a Cub landing on its front two wheels but with its tail stuck up in the air, and ground looping (this was long before the tricycle landing gear was developed).

Normally, the plane would have either gone up on its nose or completely flipped over on its back, but for some reason, it did neither. I thought to myself, "Gee, that guy is going to make a damn good pilot, or else he's extremely lucky."

To all of us who happened to see this a moment not easily forgotten, it was clear that Ray's student — Sandy — was going to be more than a Sunday afternoon pilot.

As time went by, Sandy became "one of the guys," chumming around with Ray Hylan, Pete Barton, Jim Wilmot, Baron Brodine, Gene Beattie, Dave Dutcher (a student of mine), Steve Kusak (who was immortalized as Steve Canyon's sidekick in the "Terry and the Pirates" comic strip), Vic and Eddie Evans, "Tiny" Wilmot, Dick Richards, Walt Gosnell, Jack Forsyth, Jack Jenkins, Betty Summers, George Cheatham, Russ Holderman, Howard Shafer, Tommy Greenwood, Art Collins, George Dunkelberg, Norm Pickering, Ralph Burford, Harry Gifford, Jack Ingle, Eddie Knitter,

Dave Schultz, Phil Reed, and Ray Hylan's sister, Sandy.

As with many of us, Sandy Lindsay's intense interest in flying caused a disruption in formal education. The fact that he came from one of Rochester's notable families (his grandfather was the Lindsay of the Sibley, Lindsay & Curr department stores) had no bearing on our relationship.

After passing the CAA tests, he flew at Nobadeer Airport on Nantucket under the direction of David Robb, flying passengers to the mainland. He attended Boston-Maine School of Aviation and became lifelong friends with Warren White, an instructor there.

Sandy also did his share of barnstorming all over New York State — including an unwelcome landing in the old polo field of the Country Club of Rochester (Miss Sumner, the CCR director, spent a bit of time complaining to the Rochester Airport). There was also a little excursion to Skidmore College to see Jean. She recalls that he took off in the middle of the night, buzzing the school dorm.

In June 1938, as part of a general exodus from the Rochester Airport, many pilots went to work for American Airlines. I went with the Civil Aeronautics Administration (later the Federal Aviation Administration). Two years later, on a visit to the World's Fair, I made a trip to LaGuardia and happened to run into Sandy, who was waiting to leave on a flight as a co-pilot for American. We chatted for a while and brought each other up to date on our lives.

He originally had taken a job with United Airlines at the age of 21, but American offered routes closer to home, and with his bride and family in the East, it was a logical decision to make the move.

Two weeks before Pearl Harbor, I was transferred to Rochester, and a number of months later, Sandy showed up at the airport, out of a job.

"What happened?" I asked. He replied, "After an exceptionally rough flight from LGA to Dallas, I collapsed in the locker room and American gave me a medical discharge."

He returned to instructing in the Civilian Pilot Training Program, and then went to Curtiss-Wright Aircraft in Buffalo. Sandy quickly earned a reputation as a cautious but fearless test pilot, and, because of his considerable skills, rapidly rose through the ranks to become chief production test pilot for the company.

An example of his courage was documented by Dave "Scotty" Caplan, a licensed pilot and mechanic for Curtiss-Wright who was privy to a forced landing of Sandy's. He wrote, "Sandy Lindsay was test flying a Curtiss-Wright P-47 Thunderbolt pursuit aircraft and experienced an engine fire at high altitude while checking the supercharger. He reported the plane on fire to the factory and was told to head toward Lake Erie and immediately bail out. Instead, he chose to try and save the plane from destruction and relayed his thoughts to the factory. The Niagara Falls Airport was chosen by him as the best place to land where the fire trucks were available to put out any fire."

This wasn't the only time Sandy refused to comply with orders in order to save his plane, even though it meant putting himself at great personal risk.

On another occasion, while testing a P-47, he was ordered to bail out when the engine quit cold. However, not being far from the Buffalo Airport, he stuck the nose down to maintain flying speed, and set the disabled plane down at the end of the runway.

With the loss of the hydraulic pressure, however, he had neither flaps nor brakes to slow the plane; so it rolled on and on. Finally reaching the far end of the runway, Sandy ground-looped off the runway and brought the disabled aircraft to a complete stop without a scratch. Another valuable airplane was saved to fight the war.

He and I had many radio contacts for the next year or so, but one of the more unusual ones happened in March 1944. I was pulling the midnight to 8 am watch, and except for routine matters, it was a quiet night. By 4:15 am, a raging snowstorm had developed. Suddenly I received a call — "Rochester Radio from C-46 Lindsay" — requesting clearance to land at Buffalo.

After the routine communication, I asked him, "What the devil are you doing up on a night like this?"

His reply was the standard one of the time: "Don't you know that there's a war on?"

After that, he was approached by the Civil Aeronautics Administration to test a helicopter designed by Italian designer Enea Bossi of Philadelphia. Testing was to take place at the Higgins Helicopter Testing Plant in New Orleans.

Sandy accepted the offer.

As it happened, Bossi's helicopter was ultimately unsuccessful, and Sandy elected to accept a commission as a first lieutenant with the U.S. Air Force. With his wife and 2-year-old baby, Jeannie, he traveled to Reno, Nevada, in May 1944 and was assigned to his old job of testing C-46s. However, illness struck — a brain tumor, putting an end to an exciting and wonderful career.

After several months recuperating in Rochester, Sandy was able to obtain a restricted license, permitting him to fly for his pleasure only.

In 1945, Jean and Sandy were blessed with another child, Alexander (today a lieutenant colonel in the Army). And, in 1948, James (today a United Airlines captain) was joyously greeted, as well.

During his final years, Sandy spent hours at the Rochester Airport, attending Quiet Birdmen meetings with his friends.

I ran into Jean a few years ago at the airport during the Brighton Symphony's Holiday Concert, and needless to say, we had a joyful and tearful reunion. We both knew that Sandy would want only the good times recalled — and, in that spirit, we recalled the wonderful memories of a bygone era, when individual valor, integrity, and camaraderie stood for something. Sandy had it all, but for all of us who knew him, it just wasn't for long enough.

Al Sigl and his son Paul on the "Debbie III."

Ray Porter, one of my cadets in 1942.

Sam Cooper, former Rochester International Airport director, with his crew based in Seattle Washington.

Lt. Walter Wadeikis, center, and two crew members.

Ruth Baron, killed in the Women's National Air Races in 1936.

Odds and Ends

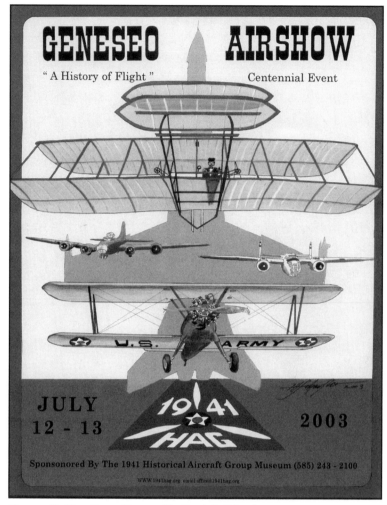

Geneseo Air Show Poster illustrated by Frank H. Schaufler

The 1941 Historical Aircraft Group, (HAG), Museum, an organization dedicated to the restoration, preservation, display and flight of aircraft on the World War II and Korean eras, as well as the recognition of all United States military personnel for their service and sacrifice. We believe the best way to display these birds of the past is... in the air!

By tradition, the annual air show is always held on the 2nd weekend in July in Geneseo, New York.

The Roswell-Elmira Connection

Stories abound about the crash of a supposed alien spacecraft in the New Mexico desert outside Roswell, New Mexico, nearly 50 years ago. But Roswell isn't alone in such out-of-this-world claims to fame.

In late summer 1953, at Chemung County Airport, Elmira, I was an employee of the Airways Operation branch of the Civil Aeronautics Administration. I suddenly got about 20 phone calls from local residents, all reporting the same unbelievable thing — "Flying saucers in the sky!"

In accordance with established procedure, these reports were immediately transmitted via intercom to Griffiss Air Force Base in Rome, New York. Next, if procedures held, five or six P-51 Mustang fighters would take to the skies to verify the reports. However, we never received any pilot feedback.

For our part, we dutifully filed our reports, which became part of official FAA records.

After about 20 minutes of UFO reports, my chief, Paul Hoskinson said, "I'll take the watch; you go see for yourself."

I left my desk at the operations office and went outside and stood looking up at the sky. At that very moment, I saw what appeared to be an aluminum disk, about 2 to 3 feet in diameter, zoom across the field, parallel to runway 24.

Upon reaching the end of the runway, the object started a climbing turn and then just disappeared, as if someone just flipped a switch.

We drew these conclusions:

- Although we had a broken cloud condition at the time, the object was below the clouds, which were estimated at about 5,500 feet.
- I couldn't classify what I saw as a physical object; it appeared to be more like a beam of light.

Over the years since, a large number of similar reports have been logged by FAA stations across the country. But there still remains no conclusive, convincing explanation for a large percentage of the sightings. The UFO question (once officially code-named Project Blue Book) remains open.

The official 1954 U.S. Navy portrait shows Sam Cooper, airport manager (second row, far left); next to him is former County Legislator John Hoff. In the background is the PBY Cooper flew extensively on submarine patrol in World War II.

Flying on the Funny Side

In the November 1988 issue of the Rochester Pilots Association newsletter, an amusing story is recounted about a small commuter airline operating in the Midwest that had a notorious reputation for its flights being late. One of the customers of this airline was a businessman who was more or less forced to depend upon this company, because no other airline served the area.

One afternoon, the businessman walked up to the ticket counter and asked, "Is your 2:30 flight on time?"

"Well, sir, as a matter of fact, it is," the agent replied.

The businessman was so elated, he said, "Son, have a cigar!"

"Keep your cigar," the agent responded. "This is yesterday's flight!"

Time Check

One of the more amusing stories making the rounds some years ago went something like this:

"Podunk Tower, from American 654, request time check, please."

Tower: "In 20 seconds coming up on 4 pm"

A few seconds later, another airline crew called, "Tower, this is United 523, correct time, please."

Tower responded: "1600, right on the button."

Another few seconds elapsed, and the new kid on the block called in for a time check: "Tower, this is Slowbird, Flight 135, request correct time, please."

Came the reply: "The big hand is on the 12, and the little hand is on the 4."

Another Tower Tale

The following took place at dusk one October day in the early '50s.

Elmira tower, on an intercom to Elmira radio: "Do you have any inbound traffic in the area?"

Ten seconds elapsed, and Elmira replied, "Negative. Only Joe Clemow in Kodak's DC-3 checked over here a few minutes ago at 6,000, en route to Rochester."

About 15 minutes later, Elmira tower called again and asked, "I suppose you want to know why I asked you if you had any inbound."

"Why?" Elmira responded.

The tower answered, "Well, I cleared Mohawk Flight 315 for take-off on Runway 24, and the pilot replied, 'You better check your traffic.' I looked around. No aircraft in sight, no radio contact with any other planes, so I called you. I then advised the pilot that we had no reported traffic in the area.

"At that point," the tower continued, "the pilot again said, 'You'd better take another look at the far end of the runway.' So, I looked down, and sure enough, there was the traffic. A herd of 35 deer was slowly sauntering across the active runway."

Flight Crew Follies

Back in the good old days, it wasn't uncommon for an airline crew to pull some prank on a stewardess embarking on her maiden flight. The following incident involved an American DC-3 en route from Newark to Albany.

The DC-3 had a small passenger door on the right side of the fuselage. When all the passengers had been boarded, the stewardess would pull the door shut, and the plane would taxi out.

For this particular flight, the pilot told the new stewardess, "Don't close the door until I personally give you orders to do so."

Unknown to the stewardess, the pilot then walked around to the other side of the DC-3, climbed up on a baggage car, and entered the cockpit through a small door on the left side of the plane.

Soon the co-pilot marched down the aisle and ordered the stewardess to haul up the door. When she protested that the pilot was the only one who could issue this order, the co-pilot replied in an angry voice, "I don't care what he told you. Pull up the door so we can get under way!"

She meekly followed his orders, the plane taxied out, and one hour and 15 minutes later, it landed at the Albany Airport. Immediately upon arriving at the gate, the pilot hopped out of the plane via the baggage door, loosened his necktie, disheveled his hair, ran around the rear of the plane, and stood there panting away.

When the stewardess lowered the door, she was stunned to find the pilot barking at her, "I told you not to close the door until I personally gave you the order. I've been running as fast as I could!"

"Where, Oh Where, Has My Clothesline Gone?"

It was July 1944. The place was Glenn Martin Airport in Baltimore, Maryland. The pilot was Ray Hylan's brother-in-law, Al Rositus, who was in the Air Force Ferry Command.

That was a beastly summer, with the temperature about 98 degrees, no wind and very little lift to the air. The destination for the flight was a bomber base in England.

The plane was a B-26, one of the 86,000 planes produced in the United States that year for ourselves and our allies. The B-26 was a low-level attack bomber with great speed and maneuverability.

One of the B-26's nicknames was "The Flying Coffin," so called because some pilots claimed the only reason engineers put wings on the plane was to carry the gas tanks. It was also called "The Flying Prostitute" because it had no visible means of support — a mere 65-foot wing span.

After being cleared for takeoff, Rositos revved up his engines, holding the plane in place with the brakes, and then quickly released them in order to gain some additional thrust. Every inch of the runway was used to coax the B-26 off the ground.

Directly off the end of the runway loomed a row of barracks, which the plane missed with only feet to spare. Just as Rositos and his co-pilot breathed a sigh of relief, the control tower called them.

"Air Force 3133, don't look now, but you just snagged a clothesline with your landing gear." Both crew members looked back and, sure enough, someone's wash was trailing behind the plane, with aprons, panties, women's stockings, and men's shirts all being torn to shreds.

I'll bet that to this day, the owner of the wash never figured who had stolen it. One could rightfully say that the "wash" ended up in the "prop wash" of a B-26 (No, Virginia, prop wash isn't a detergent for cleaning propellers).

What a way to commence an overseas flight. But, still there was a war on, and we all had to sacrifice. But a *clothesline?*

Roger Who?

A PBY was en route from Hawaii to San Diego Naval Station in April 1944. It was a Saturday night, and the skipper of the base had brought a young lady with him up to the tower.

The pilot of the PBY called in for a radio fix with the Loran System. This was a somewhat complicated triangular procedure, whereby the control tower and two stations on either side of the tower (each several miles apart) would zero in on the pilot's transmissions and then compute his exact location.

The poor pilot, who had been airborne for about 13 hours at that point, was tired, cold, and not in the best frame of mind. The controller requested, "Give me a count to 10." The pilot replied, "Roger Dodger."

The skipper grabbed the microphone from the controller and advised the pilot, "Roger will suffice!" The pilot once again replied, "Roger Dodger."

Eager to impress the young lady with his importance, the skipper then barked to the exhausted pilot, "Immediately upon landing at San Diego Base, you are hereby instructed to report to Captain Miller for disciplinary action!"

There was a 10-second pause. The pilot then fired back, "Roger Dodger, you old codger; I'm a captain, too."

World War II Words of Wisdom

"Tis better to have a WAC on your lap than a WAVE in your hair."

And Some Last Words for World War II Aviators

Remember those fleece-lined flight jackets you discarded after World War II? You can now purchase a new one from L. L. Bean for only $525. Yikes!

National Warplane Museum
17 Aviation Drive
Horseheads, NY 14845
www.warplane.org

The National Warplane Museum's 30,000 square feet Display Hanger contains restored aircraft, engines and smaller exhibits that tell the story of U.S. military aviation. Fighters, bombers and trainers from the 1930's to the 1960's are focal points of each exhibit section. (Photo courtesty of Steve Low)

One Happy Air Cadet

During March 1943, I was moonlighting as a Rochester ground school instructor in an Air Force cadet training program, in addition to my regular job in communications and airway traffic control with the Civil Aeronautics Administration at the Rochester airport.

Normally, I taught five classes per day for four weeks. An exam was given on the final day, and the results became part of the cadet's record.

On this particular Friday, I had a group of very sharp cadets from Georgia, many of whom had completed one or two years of college.

As I stood by the door collecting the test papers, one cadet turned in a sheet of paper that was blank, except for his name and 51st College Training Detachment Program.

"Where are the answers?" I asked.

"I'm sorry, sir, but I can't write," he replied.

"You can't write!?"

"I want to become a pilot," he said. "And sir, I have another problem. I need a 70 to pass, and if I fail, I'll be confined to barracks for the weekend. My girlfriend and my mother are coming up from Georgia; they'll be riding a bus for two days and I won't be able to visit with them."

I then suggested he wait at my desk while I collected the rest of the papers.

When I finished with that, I said to him, "When I called on you, you seemed to know the answers."

"Well, I know the material, but I can't write a sentence," he explained.

At that point, I gave him an oral exam and he fired back the answers. He knew every one.

"Good luck," I said. "Enjoy the weekend with your mom and girlfriend."

You've never seen such a happy cadet in your life — misty eyes and all.

Glenn H. Curtiss Museum

Above 1961 reproduction of early 1911 Curtiss Pusher. This is one of sixteen other pioneer aircraft including the "Curtiss Jenny," and WWII Flying Tigers Shark-nosed Curtiss P-40's.

Incorporated in 1961, the Glenn H. Curtiss Museum is dedicated to bringing before the public the accomplishments of early motorcycle manfacturer and aviation pioneer Glenn Curtiss. Located on Rt. 54 at Hammondsport, New York, the museum houses numerous motorcycles, aircrafts and other exhibits of Curtiss origin. In addition, the museum collection includes items of local historical significance such as boats, winemaking machinery and 19th century fire fighting equipment.

Glenn H. Curtiss Museum
8419 Route 54
Hammondsport, NY 14840
(607) 569-2160
www.linkny.com/CurtissMuseum/

A Flying Fortress and a Leprechaun

When St. Patrick's Day rolls around each year, it may be appropriate to capture the spirit of the holiday with this World War II tale.

The date: March 15, 1944. The time: 2 am. The place: Kearney Air Force Base, Kearney, Nebraska, where a briefing was held for 20 B-17 flight crews preparing for the long journey overseas to Sudbury, England.

The commanding officer informed the crews that their first stop would be a base in New England. Other flights would be joining them, coming from Salina, Kansas, and Lincoln, Nebraska.

The Air Force had blocked off the airways from 15,000 to 25,000 feet (with proper clearance from the various Airway Traffic Control centers). Each aircraft would observe radio silence until it hit the intersection of the east leg of the Buffalo Radio Range and the southwest leg of the Rochester Radio Range, known as the West Henrietta Intersection.

Rochester Radio would give an Army Flight Service advisory with the destination and an Airway Traffic Control clearance into the Boston area.

About 11 am, AF6195, with pilot Tim O'Shaughnessy at the controls, approached the intersection. He turned to his co-pilot and said, "You know, I got my pre-flight training right here in Rochester with the 51st College Training Detachment Program."

"What a coincidence," replied the co-pilot, "I did, too. Rochester Business Institute administered the program, and my instructor was Art Collins. Damn good pilot; he gave me my first spins.

"The strangest thing happened to him. He was waiting in line for a physical to get into the Air Force when a buddy in front of him decided to comb his hair and accidentally jabbed Art in the eye, permanently damaging his eye so he couldn't be commissioned as a second lieutenant."

After passing the radio fix at West Henrietta Intersection, the pilot contacted Rochester Radio and the conversation went something like this:

"Rochester Radio from AF6195 over West Henrietta Intersection, 1105 at 17,000 feet estimating Syracuse at 1126..."

"Roger, stand by" was the reply.

A moment later: "Army Flight Service advises your destination is Dow AFB, Bangor, Maine. Also, Boston ATC clears you from 25 miles west of Syracuse to Albany to maintain 17,000 feet; contact Syracuse Radio in passing and Albany Radio for clearance."

After landing at Dow Field, the crew had a 24-hour layover while they rested and their B-17G was serviced prior to the hop over the Atlantic.

At 2200 hours (10 pm), the Flying Fortress departed for Europe.

While the plane was over the North Atlantic, it ran into strong head winds and when it finally hit the Irish coast, its fuel supply was rapidly dwindling. An attempt to get a fix from a low-frequency homing device was unsuccessful and merely added to their problems.

When it became apparent that they didn't have enough fuel to reach their destination in England (the weather, in the meantime, was getting bad there, as well), the pilot, seeing a 2,000-foot strip near Dublin, decided to make an emergency landing.

Lt. O'Shaughnessy throttled back his engines to 1,200 rpm, stuck the nose down and safely landed, using up every inch of the runway. He taxied to a nearby hangar, and the co-pilot cut the switches on all four engines.

O'Shaughnessy glanced out the side window of the cockpit and looked down. What he saw was unbelievable!

There was a leprechaun staring at No. 4 engine and counting the cylinders — there were 9.

The lieutenant knew that if you could catch a leprechaun, it would bring him good luck, so he immediately unsnapped his parachute, removed his radio headset, and darted out of the plane. He then quietly crept up behind the leprechaun and threw a bear hug around the unsuspecting mythical creature.

"Let me go! Let me go! Let me go!" pleaded the leprechaun in his high-pitched voice. "If you release me, I shall grant you three wishes of your choice."

Sounds reasonable, thought the lieutenant, who eased his grip on the little fellow.

"I shall keep my promise," stated the leprechaun, "but first I must know: Who is your worst enemy?"

"No question there," said O'Shaughnessy. "At the moment, my navigator — he tried to steal my girl back in Kearney, Nebraska."

"Well, then," replied the leprechaun, "whatever I do for you, I must double for your worst enemy, so think about it."

"OK" responded the lieutenant, "it's a deal. Now my first wish...

"I would like six cartons of Chesterfield cigarettes."

The leprechaun snapped his fingers. He gave the lieutenant the six cartons and 12 for his navigator.

"Now, what is your second choice?" asked the leprechaun.

Came the answer: "One dozen nylon stockings."

The indignant leprechaun stated, "Don't you know there is a war on and these items are extremely scarce?" Nevertheless, he snapped his fingers...one dozen for the lieutenant and two dozen for the navigator.

"Now," said the leprechaun, "this is your third and final request, and I must remind you: Whatever I do for you, I shall double for your worst enemy."

The lieutenant pondered the decision and then a big grin broke across his face. With a smile from one ear to the other, he said, "I have it."

"And what is your third choice?" asked the leprechaun.

In an unhesitating voice, O'Shaughnessy replied:

"I would like my sex drive reduced by 50 percent!"

Niagara Falls - "Honeymooner's Paradise"

Recalling the good old days during the late '40's with whimsy.
Flight of three USNR "Weekend Warriors" over Niagara Falls.

A group of World War II Grumman Avengers. The planes were nicknamed "Fertile Myrtle" for obvious reasons. (Photo courtesy of U.S. Navy.)

The following is a recapitulation of the radio contact:

Flight Leader: "Sure is a pretty sight down there."

1st Wingman: "I agree, my parents honeymooned right here in Niagara Falls".

2nd Wingman: "They probably returned a second time, just to see the falls. Hee hee."

1st Wingman: "Who pulled your chain?"

Flight Leader: "Ok fellows, knock it off!"

Grand Old Days

The most successful gimmick used by the aviation industry over the years to attract crowds to the airport was to sponsor an air show, which, of course, always included a death-defying parachute jump.

Occasionally, the unexpected would occur, and on more than one occasion, the spectators enjoyed a good laugh.

One such incident occurred in Rochester in 1935.

The National Air Races always were held in Cleveland during the Labor Day weekend, and because Rochester enjoyed a fine reputation as an aviation city, many of the performers would participate here on the following weekend.

One of the stunt pilots, Art Davis, was under contract with General Motors to write "Chevrolet" as part of his skywriting displays.

Edgar "Count" Delano, who was the announcer for the show, persuaded Davis to give the Rochester Pilots Association a plug, as they were the sponsor of that year's event. It was a perfect Sunday afternoon for skywriting, a deep blue sky with very little upper winds, so the writing would hang intact for several minutes.

After completing the word "Chevrolet," Davis proceeded to write "Pilots Association." After completing the first word, "pilots," he started on the second word, "association," but after writing the first three letters, he ran out of smoke. You can picture what several hundred thousand spectators saw as they looked at the sky over Rochester.

Did Davis really run out of the flushing oil that was fed into the hot exhaust ring to produce the smoke? We never did find out, but events such as this one were part of a carefree, romantic era in aviation. This was a time when money was in short supply but fun and camaraderie abounded.

On another occasion, a beautiful, tall blonde with a rhinestone-studded tiara on her head was introduced as a visiting princess from Transylvania. The announcer informed the crowd that this would be her first airplane ride, and as thousands watched, she was escorted to a Stinson Monoplane.

The engine was already running, and, of course, the propeller was churning up quite a bit of prop wash. Just as she was about to climb into the cockpit, the prop wash from the propeller caught her long, beautiful cape. She untied the bow around her neck, and the gown was blown away. There she stood, clad only in a bra and a pair of panties. We all laughed and clapped our hands as we suddenly realized that we had just witnessed our first "aerial strip tease." We never did find out *who* put her up to it.

An air show on Irondequoit Bay in February 1934 ended in a terrible tragedy. That was the year of the coldest recorded winter in Rochester history. The temperature dropped to 23 degrees below zero, and we often had to walk three or four miles to get to school.

Baron Brodine, a mechanic for Robinson Air Service and also a parachute jumper, was the featured attraction, bringing about 10,000 spectators to the Bay. About 10 planes from the airport participated in the show, and for a while, all did a brisk job of carrying passengers at $1.50 per person.

Guy Stratton, for whom I worked, was flying our Warner-powered Fleet. During the show, there was a young fellow riding his motorcycle across the landing area being used by the planes. He was warned to leave the area but refused to heed our requests. On one approach, Stratton did a "side slip," a maneuver which enables the pilot to lose considerable altitude on approach, but the broad side of the fuselage presents the pilot with a blind spot until he levels off and prepares to land. The next thing I saw was the motorcyclist driving into the path of the landing plane, and right before my eyes, he was instantly killed. The Fleet was wrecked, standing up on its nose. Stratton climbed out, not immediately knowing what had happened.

The 10,000 spectators rushed to the scene of the accident, but they quickly dispersed when the ice started to crack. It took the next three months to repair the badly damaged plane.

In the meantime, we purchased a Waco F, which could carry two passengers at a time but never had the maneuverability of the Fleet.

Speaking of this plane, an unusual incident occurred the following year.

Shortly after soloing in our Taylor Cub, Stratton decided it was
time for me to do some spins and learn how to recover from this air-
sickening maneuver which killed more pilots in World War I than
combat.

First, let me explain that a "spin" (sometimes called a "tailspin") is
a plane out of control, headed straight down and losing a few hundred
feet per second. Having the reputation as one of the weaker stomachs
at the airport, I didn't relish this flight.

Jack Jenkins, who had only about 150 hours himself, agreed to
teach me how to recover from a spin. One problem — Jack had never
flown this type of plane himself. Nevertheless, we donned our helmets and goggles, struggled into our parachutes, and took off.

Reaching 4,000 feet, Jack called on the Gosport intercom and said,
"I'm going to do some loops and spins and a few rolls to get the feel
of the plane."

"OK," I responded as he put the plane through its paces. After
15 minutes of this, he announced, "OK, now you take over. Pull the
throttle almost all the way back, pull back on the stick, and just
before it whips down, kick hard on the right rudder. Let it do two
turns, then push the stick forward and kick left rudder to recover from
the spin."

After three or four of these stunts, my back started to warm
up, a hint that I might be on the verge of airsickness. I pulled the
throttle back and yelled, "Hey, Jack, I don't feel too well; we'd
better descend and land." He looked back at me and could see I
was getting green around the gills. He took over, landed the plane,
and we taxied up to the gas pit between hangars 1 and 2.

My fellow pilots were sitting on the benches in the operations
office, waiting to see how I made out. I unbuckled the seat belt, pushed
my goggles up on my forehead, and with the parachute still strapped
on, made a mad dash for the men's room. But I didn't make it and was
forced to "toss my cookies" into the bushes.

At that time, the airport mascot was a beautiful, brown kitten whose
favorite spot for a nap was under those bushes. How could

I have known that I would have had to stop at the exact spot she'd chosen for a snooze? She was one pitiful sight as she emerged from the bushes shaking her rear paw and looking at me with a puzzled expression as though she were saying, "What did I do to deserve this?"

As you can well imagine, everyone watching was hysterical, and sick as I was, I started to laugh. So, it's possible to be airsick and laugh at the same time. After recuperating for a half hour, I took our little friend into the locker room, and despite some mild protests, gave her a sponge bath. All was forgiven.

Trivia Questions for Old Timers...

Name the pilot flying an Aeronca whose engine quit, who fell short trying to get into the airport, landed on a car roof, and bounced over the boundary fence into the airport.

In the good old days, many of the smaller planes didn't have carburetor heaters, so when approaching in cold weather, it was essential for the pilot to hit the throttle every 10 or 15 seconds; otherwise the mixture was too lean and the engine would die.

On a blustery fall day with an 18 mph wind, John McIntee had his engine quit, and he fell short on approach to the northwest runway. His plane landed on the roof of a jalopy belonging to a Works Progress Administration (WPA) worker. It smashed in the roof and then neatly bounced over the boundary fence, safely landing on the airport with a dead engine.

When the owner of the vehicle approached his car and saw the bro-

Lt. Arthur H. Crapsey Jr. was severely injured on his final flight in a B-17 during World War II, and was awarded the Silver Star.

ken wooden slats and torn leatherette (that's what car roofs were made of in those days), he demanded $25 from the Robinson Air Service. "Robby," president of the company, offered him $10, which he gladly accepted. For $25, you could buy a pretty darn good car in those days.

During World War II, McIntee flew C-46s over the Hump in the Chinese-Burma Theater, and then settled down in Honeoye, New York.

Those who have seen the movie *Memphis Belle* had no idea how close to home the movie struck.

Art Crapsey is an active member of Citizens for a Quality Philharmonic, a support group for the Rochester Philharmonic

Orchestra. At a reception, Art mentioned that he'd been a B-17 pilot during World War II, and on his third mission over Germany, took a direct hit from a 20mm cannon. He lost part of his ankle and later had to have his leg amputated.

The 306th Bombardment Group, to which the *Memphis Belle* was attached, was the inspiration for the film *12 O'Clock High* (Art Crapsey was portrayed in the first scene) and a TV series in the early '60s.

Those interested in learning more about Lt. Crapsey's ill-fated flight should read *First Over Germany* by Russell A. Strong, published by Hunter Printing Co., Winston-Salem, North Carolina.

More Tales

The following tale made the rounds many years ago.

An American Airlines flight crew was in Rome, Italy, and decided to do some sightseeing. One of the sights they wanted to visit was the Leaning Tower of Pisa. The stewardess noticed some workers were installing a clock in the tower and asked, "Why are they installing a clock?" The captain replied, "I don't know, but it's almost noon, and they'll probably break for lunch."

Sure enough, one of the workers came down, and the stewardess asked him, "Excuse me, but why are you installing a clock?" The puzzled worker replied, "What's the sense of having the inclination if you don't have the time?" For my part, I don't believe this ever happened.

A story concerning Ray Hylan was recently brought to my attention. During World War II, Hylan had to make a trip to Florida in some miserable February weather. His instruments didn't function properly, and the radio was turned off because of all the static.

After being on instruments for three hours, one of the pilots who had come along for the ride asked Hylan, "Hey, how do you know you're headed in the right direction?" Hylan quickly responded, "We're headed south. Can't you see the temperature on the outside thermometer is rising?!"

Our Aeronautical Neighbors to the North

One of the more unusual incidents of World War II involving our Canadian allies concerned a number of young aviation cadets being trained at Island Airport in Toronto who would get lost in bad weather and wind up on the southern side of Lake Ontario.

On one occasion, a 21-year-old cadet, flying a PT19, filed a flight plan for a practice run around the Toronto area but wound up making a fuel stop in Rochester, northbound from the Southern Tier.

When I asked where he'd arrived from, he calmly answered, "Ithaca. I was lost in a snowstorm."

I pressed further, wondering aloud, "How could you wind up down in Ithaca on a flight around Toronto? Ithaca is 90 miles southeast of Rochester." The cadet confessed with a twinkle in his eyes, "My girlfriend goes to Cornell!"

On another occasion, Tommy Greenwood in the Rochester Control Tower received a frantic call from another cadet who was lost in a sudden snow squall. Greenwood asked the pilot if he could identify any object nearby.

The student pilot responded, "There's a large gas tank on the edge of the city." Greenwood gathered it was RG&E's 125-foot gas tank on Blossom Road (since removed). He advised the nervous cadet, "There's a yellow arrow painted on top of the tank, pointing to the Rochester Airport."

The student came right back, "That won't help much, I'm flying below the top of the tank." But 10 minutes later, the distraught pilot landed safely at the airport, requested a ride into Rochester and took the bus to Toronto.

Finally, those Rochesterians who visited the World's Fair at Vancouver, British Columbia, in the summer of 1986 would have seen a restored Canadian "Norseman," a single-engine monoplane powered by a Pratt & Whitney 575-hp engine and originally designed for the bush pilots flying between villages in the sparsely settled regions of northern Canada.

Because these planes carried large payloads, several were used by the Eighth Air Force in World War II. Ironically, this was the same model plane in which Glenn Miller made his final flight.

Foiled by the Royal Air Force (RAF)
using our Lend-Lease US Aircraft

Don't bother looking up the word "roadster" in the dictionary; you probably won't find it. But, way back in the '30's, it was basically a small car minus a roof.

In 1944. Col. Ralph Hayes of the 8th Air Force was given the assignment of bombing the German battleship "The Tirpitz," which was hiding in a Norwegian fjord. To accomplish this task, a modified B-17, with its superstructure removed, was converted to an open-cockpit airplane with the nickname of "The Roadster" (no roof or enclosed compartment). This open cockpit was necessary to carry two 16,000 lb. hydrostatically fused depth charges.

The strategy involved having Col. Hayes climb his remote controlled B-17 to a specified altitude, then bail out with a "mother ship" directly above directing the pilotless B-17 to crash beside the battleship.

However, the RAF knew precisely what what we were up to, sent in a squadron of Corsairs (F4U) and Wildcats (F4F) and dropped sufficient bombs to completely disable Germany's mighty battleship, which never fired a shell.

Boeing's "Sleepless in Seattle" engineers never figured on this application when designing the aircraft.

Shown in the cockpit is Col. Ralph Hayes.

Lt. Cmdr. Edward "Butch" O'Hare, 1914-1943

Where O'Hare International Got Its Name

For his efforts during World War II, Lt. Cmdr. Edward "Butch" O'Hare was awarded the Congressional Medal of Honor by President Franklin D. Roosevelt, who termed O'Hare's mission, which saved the aircraft carrier *USS Lexington* from enemy bombers "one of the most daring, if not *the* most daring, single action in the history of combat aviation."

Born in St. Louis, Missouri, on March 13, 1914, Edward Henry O'Hare attended the Naval Academy and graduated from Annapolis as an ensign in 1937. From there, he traveled to Pensacola, Florida, for flight training at the Naval Air Station and graduated in May 1940, officially qualifying as a naval aviator.

On February 20, 1942, the *Lexington*, with a crew of 1,500 men, was one of three aircraft carriers in the Pacific. When it was approximately 400 miles from its destination of Rabaul Harbor in the Solomon Islands, the carrier was spotted by a Japanese reconnaissance plane, which radioed the aircraft carrier's position before it was shot down.

Within minutes, a dozen Japanese bombers (known as "Bettys") were streaking toward the *Lexington*. Our own Navy pilots, flying F4F Wildcats, engaged the enemy and were able to shoot down six of the bombers.

Shortly, the *Lexington's* radar spotted another wave of nine Bettys. This time, six Wildcats, led by Butch O'Hare, scrambled to head off the attack. Four of the six were ordered to cover a wide sweep, while Butch and one wingman provided coverage near the carrier with the bombers less than 15 miles away.

As luck would have it, the wingman's guns jammed, and he was forced to break off, leaving Butch alone to take on the nine heavily fortified bombers.

Herbert Malloy Mason, in his book *Duel for the Sky*, best describes how O'Hare single-handedly executed a swift and decisive counterattack.

With guns blazing, he waded into the rear of the Japanese formation. Immediately, two of the bombers started smoking, their engines tore from their mountings and he watched them tumble 10,000 feet into the sea.

Butch then lined his sights on the third bomber. His .50-caliber slugs ripped into the Betty, which staggered for a moment before belching a trail of black smoke and spinning into the ocean.

At this point, his plane was in a web of tracer bullets fired by the Japanese gunners, but he ignored the deadly streams of fire being poured at him and got the fourth bomber in his sights. His guns chattered briefly, and he watched the bomber lurch from formation and spiral down to join its fallen comrades.

Now, the five remaining bombers were almost within striking distance of the *Lexington*, but Butch was determined to protect the carrier and its large crew of men. This time, as he flung his fighter head-on into the bombers, the fifth Betty blew up, spun out of control, and headed for its watery grave.

With his remaining ammunition, he sprayed the remaining bombers. At this point, the first group of Navy fighters returned to the fray — the Air Cavalry to the rescue — and provided Butch some protection by shooting down two of the four remaining bombers. The remaining two enemy planes sped for home.

In just four minutes, five Japanese planes were shot down by O'Hare, an incredible achievement at a time when Allied forces were retreating on all fronts in the Pacific Theater.

In addition to receiving the Congressional Medal of Honor, O'Hare also was awarded the Distinguished Flying Cross, the Gold Star, and the Navy Cross.

On November 21, 1943, following a night mission, he failed to return, and on November 27, 1944, he was declared dead, leaving his wife Rita, and a daughter, Kathy.

O'Hare's courage and grit under fire personified the greatness of our nation. So whenever we hear the words "Chicago O'Hare International Airport," we should think of the man behind the name — a man who gave us so much and left us too soon.

"Gentlemen, This Is It."

USS Wolverine (IX-64), one of several aircraft training carriers sailing Lake Michigan, attached to Great Lakes Naval Training Center. She is noteworthy for being coal fired , for her paddle wheels and four smoke stacks.*

In order to pass the final test before being commissioned as Naval Officers, cadets has to successfully execute six takeoffs and landings on less than a 300 foot flight deck.

*Rumor has it, there are 44 F4F's (Wildcats) on the bottom of Lake Michigan.

Blanche Scott Flying Capt. Balwin's "Red Devil" biplane.
Photo courtesy of the Glenn H. Curtiss Museum

154

Blanche Scott
the first tomboy of the sky

"Carpe diem! – Seize the day!" must have been the words racing through the mind of Greece native Blanche Scott who, as a student pilot in Hammondsport, NY, on September 2, 1910, removed the block of wood wedged under the throttle of her Curtiss Pusher Biplane and taxied out.

As she nervously pushed the throttle forward for take-off, the engine sprang to life and the plane started an erratic run across the ground. Upon reaching 22 mph, she gently pulled back on the wheel and found herself 30 feet in the air. Quickly, she pulled back the throttle, stuck the nose down and, more or less, landed the plane without sustaining any damage (much to the relief of a distraught Glenn Curtiss), thereby becoming the first aviatrix in the United States.

After a colorful career (I came to know her because she always attended the air shows at the Rochester Airport in the '30's), she became involved in radio communications. Blanche passed away in 1970.

Blanche Scott was a woman far ahead of her time; a person of great color, spirit and determination. many. Aviation buffs like to believe when her sprightly life came to an end, her soul was carried to heaven on a Curtiss Pusher, minus the wooden wedge.

In this 1955 photo, Mike Hanna and Blanche Stuart Scott swap flying stories. As a young radio personality, Mike credits Blanche with teaching him nearly everything he knew about the broadcasting business and a lot about the early days of flying. As the first woman pilot, Blanche began flying under the tutelage of Glenn Curtiss in Hammondsport, New York.

155

B-17G "Sitting Pretty"

(Approaching the white cliffs of Dover, and barely making it.)

"Answered Prayers" by Michael Short. © Michael Short. Prints available from Virginia Bader Fine Arts 1-800-233-0345 $85 each.

Answered Prayers
by Michael Short

Captain Jerry Osadnick

On the 13th of April 1944, Captain Jerry Osadnick, as a member of the 390th B-17 Bomb Group was approaching the target of the Messerschmitt factory in Augsburg, Germany, when his plane, "Sitting Pretty" was hit by flak but not seriously damaged and was able to continue the bomb run.

However on the return trip home the Group lead plane made a course correction to the left that brought them directly in the path of the Brussels, Flak area. They received a near direct burst. Number 3 engine began to smoke and lost oil pressure and would not "Feather". Number 4 engine also lost oil pressure, but was able to be feathered. Number 3 engine windmilled. When Jerry tried to increase power to number 1 and 2 engines only number 1 would respond making it very difficult to maintain altitude and formation losing 700 ft. per minute.

The tail gunner was very seriously wounded, which prevented his bailing out. It was decided the entire crew would stay with the plane and radioed Air Sea Rescue and advised they would ditch about 2 miles short of the Dover coast. Air Sea Rescue dispatched 2 boats and advised they would wait for the crew.

The aircraft was hit by flak again between Ostend and Dunkirk. They kept going as they approached the White Cliffs of Dover, two P-47's of the 375th Fighter Group appeared and escorted them in.

Capt. Jerry Osadnick miraculously was able to maintain sufficient altitude to safely land at Manston. As they landed number 3 propeller fell off the plane!!

The tail gunner was hospitalized for 2 months but recovered to be able to complete his tour of missions. He still walks with a limp. He was recently awarded a long awaited DFC.

Capt. Osadnick flew his 29 missions over Nazi-held Europe and received the Distinguished Flying Cross with 1 Oak Leaf Cluster, and the Air Medal with 4 Oak Leaf Clusters. Upon completion of flying his missions he was assigned to the 312th ferrying Squadron in the UK.

Jerry who lives in Fairport, New York, is a member of the Geriatric Pilot's Association, and The Experimental Aircraft Association. He is also on the Board of Directors of the 390th Bomb Group Veterans Association and a Life Member of the 390th Memorial Museum Foundation in Tucson, Arizona.

Diploma

390 th. BOMB GROUP

This is to Certify that **J.A. OSADNICK** a member of WITTAN'S WALLOPER BOMBING COLLEGE HAS SUCCESSFULLY COMPLETED HIS TOUR OF OPERATIONS AGAINST HITLER'S HOT SHOTS AND IS NOW ELIGIBLE TO RETURN TO GOD'S COUNTRY (THE LUCKY BASTARD)

Missions Completed

1. Kiel. gr.
2. Bremen. gr.
3. Onoeux. Fr.
4. Kiel. gr.
5. Ludwigshafen, gr.
6. Frankfurt. gr.
7. Brunswick. gr.
8. Wilhelmshaven, gr.
9. Frankfurt. gr.
10. Villacoublay, Fr.
11. Romilly-Sur-Seine, Fr.
12. Brunswick, gr.
13. Rostock. gr.
14. Hanover. gr.
15. Berlin, gr.
16. Berlin, gr.
17. Berlin, gr.
18. Brunswick, gr.
19. Augsburg, gr.
20. Cazaux, Fr.
21. Ludwigshafen, gr.
22. Quakenbruck, gr.
23. Maldegem, Belg.
24. Rostock, gr.
25. Leipzig, gr.
26. Augsburg, gr.
27. Werl, gr.
28. Wizernes, Fr.
29. Laon-Athies, Fr.
30.

PROFESSOR OF BOMBING

Robert O. Good

DEAN OF FORMATION

Aviation High Jinks: Fact and Fiction

Allen Brown in 1944, when he was 18 years old. He is the husband of Marion Brown, Brighton town clerk.

A few years ago, Al Brown, a neighbor who was a tail gunner on a B-17 during World War II, questioned whether all of the aviation high jinks I'd written about over the years actually could have happened.

"What? Make this stuff up?" I told Al that I was amazed and intrigued by the idea that anyone could concoct such stories and that I was always a participant, observer, or a correspondent regarding the various incidents I wrote about.

But that set me to thinking — had I missed my calling as a fiction writer? So, in deference to my friend Al and other skeptics, I leave you to decide for yourselves which of the two following aviation adventures is the real McCoy. And remember: Truth is always stranger than fiction.

Tale No. 1

One of the perks of being a grease monkey at the airport back in the '30s was having the responsibility of sitting in the open cockpit of a biplane and warming up an engine in the bitter cold. When the oil temperature of the engine reached 80 degrees, we would open the throttle wide, and the restrained plane would shake as if it were about to take off. Of course, the wheels were blocked, but when I was a 15-year-old, my dreams were reinforced that someday I would fly.

However, there was one pilot at the airport who generally scoffed at thoroughly warming up an engine in cold weather, and this little quirk almost did him in.

In the fall of 1936, Ray Hylan acquired a Waco cabin plane with a 225-horsepower Wright Whirlwind engine. Ray had a regular clientele who, on the spur of the moment, would call up and ask if they could charter a flight. Such was the case on one mild, clear evening that fall, when Ray and his passenger were departing for Utica with the temperature hovering around 50 degrees. An hour later, Ray dropped off his passenger and waited for him to return later that night.

The passenger returned around 11:30 pm, and the two prepared to fly on to Newark, New Jersey. Ray started the engine, taxied out, and immediately took off. But during Ray's wait, the temperature had dropped below 30 degrees. Because it was fall, the aviation oil (the heaviest, used in summertime, was still in the crankcase) was so thick that the oil pressure shot up and burst the oil line. All the oil gushed out, and the engine seized up and quit.

Plucky Ray was able to make a "dead stick" (dead engine) landing and set the plane down next to the Erie Canal in total darkness.

After the plane traveled about 150 feet, it struck a pipeline connecting the canal to a huge storage tank located about 200 feet from the canal bank. The pipe, which was about 2 feet above the ground, proved to be an unmovable obstacle when the plane's landing gear was sheared off and some damage was done to the cowling. Poor Ray sustained some facial cuts and bruises.

After emergency room treatment, he returned to the accident scene to survey the damage. What he saw really shook him up.

He recalled, "I looked around, and there, no more than 300 feet from where I cracked up, was a high-voltage transmission line, and I don't know whether I flew under those wires or over them because I never saw them to begin with."

With Ray's death several years ago, an era came to an end. But thank goodness, we have Hylan Drive and the Raymond P. Hylan Mathematics Building at the University of Rochester to remind us what a charitable and benevolent person he was.

Tale No. 2

During World War II, a contingent of more than 2,000 women pilots in the Air Transport Command provided outstanding service for the war effort by ferrying P-51s, P-39s, P-38s, P-47s, P-63s, and B-17s to various ports of embarkation around the country.

The Women Air Service Pilots (WASP) were commanded by Jacqueline Cochran. In recent years, Congress enacted a law that granted them all the rights and privileges of other officer personnel of World War II, a long overdue recognition of their outstanding efforts in the successful battle of survival during that conflict, but no officer commissions.

In the fall of 1946, a former WASP pilot, I'll call her Hilda, was walking her dog along the shore at Asbury Park, New Jersey. She happened to notice a bottle washed up on shore. Curious, she picked it up, examined it closely, and then removed the cork.

And what do you suppose happened?

An elated genie popped out, extremely jubilant over his new-found freedom. He then turned to Hilda and declared, "Because you have freed me from my imprisonment, I am going to grant you three wishes."

Hilda was ecstatic over the offer and exclaimed, "Let me go into a holding pattern for a minute," and then pondered the offer. After a few minutes she said, "My first request would be for a new three-bedroom beach home right on that bluff behind us. It should come complete with a new high-fidelity record player, including all three speeds — 78, 45, and 33 rpm."

The genie snapped his fingers and, lo and behold, she took possession of her new home.

"And what is your second choice?" the genie asked.

Hilda thought for a moment and replied, "I would like to have an AT6 (Advance Trainer) with 575-horsepower Pratt and Whitney engine, which I have flown many times."

The genie replied, "Well, I have to check with the War Surplus

Section of the government and will be right back." A few minutes later, he returned and sadly informed her that the last one had just been sold to a pilot in Rochester, New York, named John Kendall, who had served as a flight instructor with Page Airways during the war. However, he added, "There are a few P-51 Mustangs still available at $3,500 each."

Hilda excitedly exclaimed, "I'll take one, but make sure it is one of the late models fitted with a Rolls-Royce engine instead of the Allison, since the Rolls is a far better performing airplane at high altitudes." (You can still buy a P-51, but bring along a certified check for $1,000,000 plus).

Within two minutes, the genie returned with the P-51 of her choice, and then asked, "Hilda, what is your third and final choice?" She thought for a moment and then replied, "I would like you to transform my dog into a handsome young man and have him marry me."

Without batting an eyelash, the genie made the transformation took place, a minister appeared, and the ceremony was performed.

Hilda then turned to her new husband and stated, "I would like to have you pick me up in your arms, carry me into our new home, and make passionate love to me."

He gazed into her expectant eyes and mournfully apologized. "I'm terribly sorry, but I can't grant your request."

"And why not?" she demanded.

And her new husband responded: "Remember when I was a puppy? You had me neutered!"

Whatever the Year, the Public Responds to Tragic Accidents

By spanning of the Atlantic Ocean in 1927, Charles Lindbergh provided the spark for the birth of a number of today's major airlines, including TWA, which began operations as a mail carrier.

Ironically, a key player in the growth and development of U.S. naval aviation and TWA was Capt. D.W. "Tommy" Tomlinson, USNR, who grew up in Batavia, a mere 13 miles from nearby Churchville, the home of Capt. Stephen Snyder (the TWA pilot who died along with 229 others aboard Flight 800). Prior to TWA's fatal accident, in the course of U.S. airline history, two other accidents occurred that greatly impeded the expansion of the industry.

In 1931, Knute Rockne of the University of Notre Dame, who many considered the greatest college football coach of all time, died when a Fokker TriMotor crashed in stormy weather, killing all aboard. The accident occurred when instrument flying was virtually unheard of, radio aids to navigation were minimal, and pilots basically flew by the seat of their pants. As a result, a dismal pall settled on this infant industry as would-be passengers refused to fly. However, because of the airmail subsidies from the federal government, the airlines managed to survive, followed by a period of slow expansion beginning in 1932.

With the financial assistance of Harry Guggenheim, the Bureau of Standards, Sperry, Pioneer and Kollsman, various instruments were introduced, which made "flying blind" possible. One of the most important was Sperry's Automatic Pilot, perfected in 1932, which enabled Harold Gatty and Wiley Post to fly around the world in eight days. The following year, Post, using the same plane, the *Winnie Mae*, duplicated the feat alone and became a world hero in his own right.

On August 29, 1933, thousands of Rochesterians gathered at the Rochester Airport to see Post.

Although Post grew up in Texas, he worked most of his life in the oil fields of Oklahoma, and through an unfortunate accident, lost

163

sight in one eye. With the compensation, he purchased his own airplane, did a lot of barnstorming, and during his adventures met up with a homespun philosopher named Will Rogers, who also enjoyed an outstanding reputation as vaudeville actor, comedian, movie actor, and radio personality.

In the summer of 1935, the scheduled passenger airlines suffered another setback when Post and Rogers were killed near Point Barrow, Alaska, when their Lockheed Orion, equipped with floats, crashed shortly after takeoff. The great Irish tenor, John McCormack, noted, "A smile has disappeared from the lips of America." The entire nation went into a period of mourning. Investigation provided no logical explanation of the probable cause.

Captain D.W. Tomlinson, USN

Wives refused to permit their husbands to use the airlines for business trips, and to add to the woes of the air carriers, the first B-17 delivered to the Army Air Corps at Wright Field, Dayton, Ohio, took off with the controls locked, killing all on board. An entire year elapsed before a second B-17 was available. This time, Capt. Tommy Tomlinson was assigned to serve as a check pilot for the flight.

Tomlinson, who was an aeronautical engineer, graduated from the U.S. Naval Academy in 1917 and the Navy Flight School in Pensacola, Florida, in 1921. He played an important role in the development of dive bombing and qualified on the *USS Langley* as a pilot. In 1928, he helped create the famous Navy demonstration team, "The Three Seahawks," which took top honors at the National Air Races in Los Angeles.

After resigning from the Navy in 1929, he became a commercial pilot, starting as vice president of operations at Maddux Airlines flying the night mail, passengers, and stratospheric research, as Maddux was incorporated into TWA's structure. As a member of the technical committee, he dissuaded TWA from purchasing tri-motor planes and worked with Douglas Aircraft in developing the DC-1, for which he served as a co-pilot.

The prototypes set many American and world speed records and successfully flew on one engine. They were quickly followed by the development of the DC-2, which TWA was the first to acquire, followed by American, United, Eastern, and many foreign airlines. Because the DC-2 was only a 14-passenger plane, within a relatively short time the now famous DC-3 (C-47) made its appearance. The rest is history.

During 1936, in a move designed to boost air travel in winter, American inaugurated a program providing free fare for wives accompanying their husbands on business trips. After a month's trial, officials sent out questionnaires to the wives for comments on the promotion.

The reaction was somewhat devastating as many wives responded: "What flight?! I never took a trip with my husband." So much for American's great promotion!

Tomlinson became chief engineer for TWA in 1936, and performed much of the research and development that went into the design of the Boeing four-engine "Stratoliner," and flew the first plane accepted by TWA.

Following several years of active duty in the Navy during World War II, Tomlinson returned to TWA and became deeply involved in developing the design and specification for the Lockheed "Constellation," an airplane that became a dominant transport plane until the arrival of the jets.

WASPs pose at air field on U.S. soil. Dawn Rochow Seymour is third from right.

Flying With Honor

Like millions of others, Dawn Rochow's interest in aviation was piqued by Charles Lindbergh's historic non-stop flight from New York to Paris in May 1927. Her fascination with airplanes was further heightened by the exploits of Amelia Earhart, the first woman to fly across the Atlantic.

Dawn graduated from Pittsford High School as valedictorian of her class, received a Bachelor of Science degree from Cornell University in 1939, and stayed on as an instructor.

In 1939, with war clouds threatening, President Roosevelt established the Civilian Pilot Training Program to create a reservoir of trained pilots as the country moved closer to war with the invasions of foreign soil by German, Italian, and Japanese armies in the '30s.

Dawn was the first woman to complete the CPT program at Cornell and in late 1939 soloed with an old colleague of mine, Herb Peters, as her instructor at the old Ithaca Airport. In 1940, she earned her private pilot's license. Ironically, Willard Straight (Cornell class of 1901) wrote a letter to his infant son fearing that when he left to serve in World War

I, he would never see the child again. Straight died in France in 1918, but the words to his son are now inscribed over the fireplace in Willard Straight Hall:

Dawn Seymour graduated from Cornell University in 1939.

"Treat all women with chivalry. The respect of your fellows is worth more than applause. Understand, sympathize with those who are less fortunate than you are. Make up your own mind, but respect the opinion of others. Don't think anything right or wrong because someone tells you so. Think it out yourself, guided by the advice of those whom you respect. Hold your head high and keep your mind open. You can always learn."

In 1943, Dawn demonstrated her chivalrous nature by joining the WASPs (Women's Air Service Pilots), an arm of the U.S. Air Force. Her first assignment was Avenger Field, Sweetwater, Texas, followed by ferrying group training, and then four-engine transition certification as a B-17 first pilot at Fort Myers, Florida.

In a letter to her family on September 18, 1944, she wrote: "Have been having a wonderful time flying 'Big Friend,' as we call the B-17" (she and other WASPs ferried these planes to various bases in the continental United States).

"The other day, I made the best landing of my whole flying career. For about 45 minutes, a big rain cloud just sat over the field to the very boundaries. And when I came in, the runway was still wet. I leveled out just right and she settled — no bounce, no bump, not even a squeak. Just as smooth as silk ... why, we didn't even know we were on the ground. I was tickled pink. One in a million ... Wilkie, my co-pilot, said: 'I'll be glad when you women leave and quit showing up us men' (and he winked)."

Dawn flew many other types of aircraft and served as a co-pilot on B-26s on tow target missions. Many of her fellow WASPs flew everything from PT-13s to B-29s, in many cases freeing up the male pilots for combat duty.

Unfortunately, 37 WASPs were killed in various accidents while helping their country toward final victory.

Dawn Seymour and her husband, Morton, now reside in Naples, New York, and spend their winters in Tucson, Arizona.

They have two sons, three daughters and eight grandchildren.

Back in the '30s, the Chamber of Commerce touted a slogan:

Dawn Seymour, far left.

"Rochester-Made Means Quality." It applied not only to our large clothing industry, but also to such firms as Kodak, Bausch & Lomb, and Taylor Instruments. But this view could justifiably be expanded to include the high degree of accomplishment in training pilots for the military and scheduled airline operations.

Among the thousands of pilots who received part of their military training at the Rochester Airport, Lt. Raymond Porter, USNR, was among the finest. Upon graduation from John Marshall High School, Ray attended Buffalo State University and received his degree in 1940. In the fall of 1942, Ray joined the Navy for training as a pilot and, for a brief period, received his ground school instruction through a CPT program conducted by Rochester Business Institute (where he was one of my students) and his flight training with Rochester Aeronautical Corp., owned by Peter Barton.

Upon completion of his flight training, Ray was assigned to the Pacific as the pilot of the famous Mariner PBM flying boat. The Mariner was part of a squadron of patrol bombers, attached to the seaplane tender, *USS Chandeleur*, and played an important role in the invasion of Okinawa.

Among the many battles Ray was engaged in, on one occasion both engines of his PBM quit at 2,000 feet. Without power, the PBM had the glide ratio of a truckload of bricks. Ray dove for the ocean to maintain flying speed, and flattened out at the last moment, plunking the plane onto the surface of the Pacific, only popping some rivets. Only one crew member suffered an injury — a slight cut on the forehead.

Ray, who is modest to a fault, hesitates to discuss his contributions to the war effort; however, he was the recipient of four air medals and the Distinguished Flying Cross, for which James Forrestal, Secretary of the Navy, cited "his gallant devotion to duty in keeping with the highest traditions of the United States Naval Service."

After the war, Ray spent 20 years as an FBI special agent and 15 years as chief of Eastman Kodak's security department. Ray passed away last year and is survived by "Tinzie," who lives in Penfield, New York, five children and eight grandchildren.

Delivering Air Mail the Old-fashioned Way

Air mail pick-up system.

"Did Sally Rand and her fan help spawn the birth of USAir?" Skeptical shoppers seeing this tabloid headline at the supermarket checkout would probably chalk this up to another ridiculous attention-getter. But there's an element of truth in this headline.

Old-timers will recall the Chicago World's Fair, which opened in 1933 at the height of the Depression. It was a financial fiasco until this country and the rest of the world discovered Sally Rand and her fans.

Rocketed into instant limelight and glory, she was seen by millions who flocked to the Fair to witness her and her intriguing dance, thereby saving the enterprise from certain financial doom and bankruptcy.

Hardly anyone at the Fair noticed the patented invention of Dr. Lytle S. Adams of Chicago. Adams' invention was a complex system "comprised of hooks, cables, safety releases, shock absorbers, and winches [which] enabled an airplane to pick up and deliver mail sacks without having to land."

However, a glider pilot named Richard C. DuPont from Wilmington, Delaware, witnessed a demonstration of this Rube Goldberg contraption and was immediately caught up with the potential of this unique device.

Wheels started spinning in his head. Wow! An airmail pickup and delivery system for isolated communities throughout the United States!

Six years later, on May 12, 1939, under DuPont's leadership, All-American Aviation (commonly referred to as AAA or Triple A) made its maiden flight to Latrobe, Pennsylvania, from Pittsburgh, simultaneously picking up a mail pouch suspended between two poles while releasing another pouch. Thank you, Sally Rand, for breathing life into the failing World's Fair and consequently enabling this small airline to get off the ground (pun intended).

With operations under way in West Virginia, Delaware, Ohio, and Jamestown, New York, the airline, which started with five Stinson Reliants powered by 260-horsepower Lycoming engines, quickly cut a niche for itself in aviation history.

Basically, the pickup system consisted of two poles approximately 20 feet off the ground with a wire strung between them, to which the mail pouch to be picked up was attached.

The plane would make an approach at about 90 mph, coming down to 25 feet above the ground. It would snag the pickup pouch, while, at the same time, the clerk aboard would kick the delivery pouch out the door.

The sight of this operation was permanently ingrained in any observer's mind.

The stories of those who flew the Stinsons are innumerable.

Many times, when the scheduled airlines would cancel because of inclement weather, the airmail systems would continue to operate.

A pilot would have to make his drops and pickups in valleys near Bellefonte, Pennsylvania, and then fly over mountain tops hidden in the clouds.

Prior to his departure from Pittsburgh, the pilot would measure off one inch on a cigarette and mark it with a pen. Upon leaving the valley, he would light the cigarette, climb over the mountain, flying blind, and when the cigarette burned to the line, he would begin his descent into the next valley, break out of the clouds, and make another delivery.

Such were the high-tech aviation techniques of 50 years ago!

In 1948, AAA was granted authority to become a feeder line carrier and was given one year to phase out its exclusive airmail service. Its name was to become Allegheny Airlines.

But let's retrace our steps a bit. Back in 1945, Robinson Air Lines began operations in Ithaca with a fleet of Fairchild 24s, each capable of carrying two passengers. Robinson concentrated its efforts between Ithaca and Roosevelt Field, a distance of 173 miles.

Shortly after the war, Robinson picked up some Cessna UC78s and later a few twin-engine Beechcraft C45s. Because of expansion, the airline changed its name to Mohawk Airlines.

During this time, an undergraduate at the University of Rochester who enjoyed playing the violin wanted to play in a university orchestra. None existed at that time, but he managed to become a member of one of the orchestras of the Eastman School of Music. His name was Ed Colodny, who came from Burlington, Vermont.

In 1972, after a prolonged strike by Mohawk pilots, the airline merged with Allegheny Airlines and changed its name to USAir to reflect that it was now an international carrier and no longer a regional airline.

USAir eventually acquired several airlines, including Lake Central, Empire, and Pacific Southwest (later Piedmont).

In 1988, it carried 62 million passengers, a remarkable record. And that violinist, Ed Colodny, who played in the Eastman School Orchestra? He went on to become president and chairman of the board of USAir, which renamed itself USAirways in early 1997.

"A Sky High Romance"

Michael C. "Mike" Hanna spent 31 years with American Airlines. Originally from Rochester, he and his ex-flight attendant wife, Hazel, live in Livingston County. Beginning flying in 1952 at the Dansville (NY) Airport, with lessons from A.A.'s E.M. "Gene" Beattie, Hanna earned his license in '53 from the Ray Hylan School of Aeronautics in Rochester.

Crisscrossing the United States, Mike flew a host of personalities from Bob Hope and Dolly Parton to Pink Floyd, Chet Atkins, Liza Minnelli and Ernie Banks. *(Photo by Don Sylor)*

Hired by American a year after her future husband Mike began, Hazel Haynes Hanna saw the end of the piston aircraft and the introduction of many newer turbojets. Their marriage perhaps was made in heaven but certainly began at 35,000 feet when they first met! Now a "kiwi," Hazel still keeps in touch with many of her "stewardess" friends. (1966 A.A. Flt. Academy photo)

Rendition of a Curtiss T-32 Condor at Buffalo Airport during a blizzard done by artist Robert Parkes.

Surviving a Wintry Plane Crash

Luck truly was a "lady" the night of December 28, 1934, when an American Airlines Curtiss Condor biplane flown by Capt. Ernest Dryer made a forced landing on the side of a snow-covered Adirondack mountain 12 miles northeast of Little Falls, New York, northeast of Utica. Dryer "pancaked" the disabled aircraft onto a mountain slope, saving the lives of all four occupants.

It was so unusual for a nighttime plane crash on the side of a mountain to have a happy ending that this one held my attention for 63 years.

I was an 18-year-old "grease monkey" at the Rochester Flying School when the crash occurred.

Recently, after 65 years in the aviation business, I went to Little Falls and Herkimer to research the crash in newspaper, museum and library files. From them, I've fleshed out an account, imagining the dialogue among those involved.

The flight of the 14-seat plane had originated in Boston en route to Cleveland, but because of foul weather it landed at Syracuse. After refueling, it departed for Albany with a scheduled air-mail stop at

Utica.

With Utica reporting a 200-foot ceiling, and 5-mile visibility and heavy snow, the flight entered a holding pattern on the east leg of the Syracuse radio range, waiting for improved weather.

Suddenly, Dale Dryer, Ernie's brother and co-pilot, muttered, "Dammit!" Snow static had wiped out the radio signals.

As the plane droned on, the accumulation of heavy snow on the wings made the controls a little mushy. At 10:41 pm, the crew radioed that they were bypassing Utica and proceeding to Albany. But shortly afterward, the right engine carburetor iced up and died. And with ice forming on the wing's leading edges, a crash landing seemed imminent.

With the Condor losing 300 feet per minute, both pilots desperately began looking for a clearing — a lake, any place to set down.

Suddenly as a wooded area loomed directly ahead, Ernie barked, "Cut the switches!"

With a speed of 120 mph, Ernie pulled the aircraft into an 85-degree vertical climb to be parallel to the mountainside. Dale read off the airspeed: 90-75-60-30-5-0. The plane stalled out and momen-

Photo of American Airways Condor crash in the Adirondacks taken December 30, 1934. Note survivors waving at the rescue plane.

tarily slid back on its tail. Then the nose plunged down, smacking the treetops with a tremendous wallop and smashing the lower wings before settling down into the trees and coming to rest on a mountain slope, 400 feet above the base and several hundred feet below the peak.

Sitting in complete darkness and stunned but grateful for surviving one of the most phenomenal landings in aviation history, Ernie turned to Dale and asked, "Are you OK?" Dale, with a badly bruised jaw, only nodded.

The other two occupants, an American co-pilot "dead-heading" (hitching a ride to a terminal to pick up plane) and another passenger, were unhurt. Ernie bellowed, "Let's get the hell out of here before this damn thing catches fire!"

Fortunately, that didn't happen.

With the temperature at 25 below zero and only two blankets among them, the four huddled together against the cold. The only provisions aboard were two Hershey bars. But they survived the night.

By midnight, American's Albany office notified the State Police and the media that one of its planes was missing. Search teams were organized.

But the next day, three more feet of snow prevented any searching. However, J.R. Brown, the American co-pilot aboard for the ride, repaired the broken antenna, and before the battery went dead, radioed Albany: "We are down but OK and probably north of our course. Please notify our families."

Some 36 hours after the crash, the weather cleared, allowing three Schenectady pilots, Marvin "Pee Wee" Horstman, Edward Haven, and Lawrence "Skip" Wiecynsky, along with 35 other planes, to search the Mohawk Valley and several miles north. A General Electric engineer in Schenectady rigged up a mobile radio in a police car to maintain communication between the search planes and Albany.

Some of the planes flew over the wreckage, but none of the pilots spotted it. On the ground, the four survivors, frost-bitten, hungry and weak, began to despair of ever being rescued.

Shortly before sunset, 44 hours after the crash, Capt. Dryer came up with a plan: toss fabric from the plane wings and gasoline from the tanks onto their small bonfire just as a search plane passed overhead.

And, sure enough, an American Airlines pilot flying a Stinson Reliant caught a glimpse of the black smoke trail and shoved the throttle wide open, dropped one wing into a tight 90-degree vertical bank and raced toward the wisp of smoke some four miles away.

Wide open, he dove down directly into the thin column of smoke and through the tall trees and spotted the wreckage — and the four survivors wildly waving their arms. Twice he rocked his wings, and "goosed" the engine by opening and closing the throttle to signal he'd spotted them.

He executed one more pass, this time with the propeller in flat pitch (which set up one helluva roar), and with his speed hitting 150 mph, he headed for Albany, since his plane had no radio.

But within five minutes he encountered another American Condor flown by Capt. Dean Smith, one of the pilots who had flown Admiral Byrd over the South Pole.

He beckoned Smith to follow him. As both planes zoomed over the wreckage, Smith radioed the wreck's exact location to Albany.

Within minutes, two National Guard planes left Albany for the scene

Marv "Pee Wee" Horstman, left, with the plane he used to search for the downed Condor.

where they dropped flares, food supplies, medicine, and blankets. However, none of the downed men had the strength to retrieve the air drops.

Meanwhile, a search party — eight woodsmen and guides led by Lester Pertello, set out for Wilder Mountain, roughly 12 miles northeast of Little Falls. In his report, Pertello subsequently wrote: "We were all on snowshoes — could not have reached them if we hadn't been, since the snow was waist deep in many places."

At one point, Lester fired his rifle three times, and Ernie responded once with his .38-caliber handgun (a carryover from Pony Express days when any-one transporting the mail had to carry a gun).

Marv Horstman, chief pilot for TWA.

Near the top of the mountain, Pertello found all four men huddled around their small fire. As he tells it, "All were shaking badly from the cold, too weak to talk above a whisper. They said they'd given up hope of rescue, even after they'd seen the planes."

Pertello and another member of the search party, Floyd Kreutzer, stayed with them, providing blankets and food while the others fetched toboggans and bobsleds to bring them out, because they did-

n't have the strength to walk. It took five hours to bring them to safety and 12 more before they reached St. Elizabeth's Hospital in Utica.

Luck was with those men that fateful, bitter night, but Capt. Ernest E. Dryer proved himself a hero whose exceptional skills and courage in such devastating cir-cumstances assures him a permanent place in aviation history.

Ernie Dryer

(Left) Christopher S. Geiselmann, the associate curator of the Glenn H. Curtiss Museum in Hammondsport, NY. A USAF Vietnam veteran, he had the privilege of playing the part of Glenn Curtiss in the PBS Series "War Ships"...

Pictured above is part of the engine cowling of the American Airlines Curtiss Condor that crashed 15 miles northeast of Little Falls, NY, on December 28, 1934, part of the exhibit at the museum.

(Right) Denise Weldan of Ithaca, NY

Recalling the Thrill of Flying

As the Great Depression of the '30s strangled this country's economy, a young intrepid aviator named Ray Hylan started his own flying service at the Rochester Airport.

In those days, he had to wait in the rear of a tailor shop on Chili Avenue while his only suit was pressed. Yet, through skill, shrewdness, and a sense of fair play, Ray became one of the largest dealers of Piper aircraft in the country. He built a series of flying schools in Binghamton and Utica, and, of course, the largest in Rochester, New York.

In his book *Fate is the Hunter*, Ernest Gann spoke of the heavy air traffic at the Rochester Airport in the late '30s and early '40s. More than 50 percent of Rochester's air traffic was generated by Hylan, with the balance accounted for by the Robinson Air Service, Rochester Flying School, and the Rochester Aeronautical Corp.

Gerald Wilmot, left, with Najeeb Halaby and Sheldon "Torchy" Lewis, formerly from Elmira.

Shortly after Pearl Harbor, Ray and Jim Wilmot (once a manager of the Rochester Airport) got a contract to establish one of the largest primary flight schools for the Army Air Corps in Louisiana, where thousands of cadets received their training.

Hylan Flying Service closed around 1987 because of high insurance rates. Upon his death a few years ago, it was estimated that Ray's wealth was $30 million.

During our numerous conversations with him during the twilight years of his life, he always spoke of the "good old days," namely the '30s, when romance in aviation was alive and well, when pilots wore helmets and goggles, and young ladies still admired the reckless young men and their flying machines.

As an active participant in this area, I was privy to Ray's

experiences during this golden era of aviation, and some are well worth recalling.

During the fall of 1933, Ray operated two Waco Fs, and, on occasion, I would barnstorm with him. On one such event, Dick Richards, Elmer Page, and I were packed into the front cockpit of the plane for an air show at Brizee Field on Marsh Road in the Village of Pittsford.

Because there was to be a parachute jump by Ray Moulton, hundreds of people flocked to the free event. As a result, parking space was at a premium. One spectator parked his Ford jalopy in the tall grass on the south side of the field, only a few hundred feet from the power lines bordering the airport.

Business was brisk that afternoon. On one takeoff, Ray held down the nose of his plane, intending to pull straight near the end of the field.

He never saw the jalopy hidden in the grass, and then "BOOM!" — the right wheel of his plane crashed through the windshield of the unoccupied car, tearing its roof open.

The plane literally stopped in midair with the power lines looming up ahead. Ray somehow hauled the plane over the wires, missing them by inches, stuck his nose down to regain flying speed, brought the plane around, and landed.

He immediately hopped out of the cockpit, kicked the right wheel with his foot, and barked at the three of us, "OK, you guys, start sellin' those rides again!"

I never learned the reaction of the car owner when he returned to find his vehicle demolished.

Ray was never one to pass up a chance to make a buck. When he went barnstorming to Hornell, Penn Yan, and other regions, he would carry passengers until the last minute and then return to Rochester, without lights, and land perhaps as much as an hour after sunset.

Inspector Jack Sommers, who admired Ray considerably, warned him on two occasions that flying after sunset without navigation was a violation of civil air regulations.

As the saying goes, "The time comes when patience ceases to be a virtue." Ray returned one Sunday evening about an hour past sunset and found Sommers waiting for him.

When Ray landed, Sommers told him, "OK, Ray, I warned you. Now I'll take your license." Ray was grounded for the first time in his life.

When a friend told Ray, "I've got connections in Washington. I'll get your license back," Ray said, "Go ahead."

A few days later, Sommers got a call from Washington regarding a report on the incident: "Where was the license?"

Jack Jenkins

Sommers had intended to hold Ray's license for only a few days, but he was so infuriated by this political move that he sent Ray's license to Washington, recommending it be suspended for 60 days, which was upheld.

But Ray remained unfazed. At that point, Jack Jenkins, Dick Richards, and Elmer Page handled the charter part of the operation.

As the charter trips developed, Page, who held a limited commercial license (restricted to 50 miles from Rochester), would occupy the left seat of the Stinson S, Ray the right seat, their passengers behind them.

An American Airlines first; captain and first officer John Jenkins, Sr. and John Jenkins, Jr. John, Sr.'s father, Jack, also flew for American, marking three generations of John Jenkinses flying for the airline.

Nobody ever questioned whether Elmer exceeded the 50-mile limit — Ray took a generous view of what constituted a mile. The result was that no charter revenue was lost by the suspension.

With the closing of Hylan Flying School, an era came to an end. And when it's occasionally suggested that the Rochester International Airport be renamed to honor a distinguished citizen, throwing the name "Hylan International Airport" into the hopper isn't too farfetched.

Some Close Calls

Back in 1932, an American Airways Stinson Tri-Motor landed at Albany Airport. Just as it touched down, the pilot heard a crunching sound at the rear of the plane and it was dragged to an early stop.

Removing his flashlight from the cockpit, the pilot got out of his plane and walked toward the tail section. And guess what he saw? Another pilot climbing out of a single engine Monocoupe! The latter had never seen the airliner and had landed directly on the tail of the Stinson, badly damaging both planes. The Monocoupe had no lights on, control towers were non-existent, and fortunately nobody was injured in the collision.

In the winter of 1934, Pete Barton, who operated Rochester Aeronautical Co., had a charter flight to Lake Placid. As part of the weekend festival at the Lake Placid Club that weekend, a competition of horse-drawn sleighs was held. Two poles with a steel wire between them were erected, with a white flag to mark the finish line for the race.

The following morning, Barton and his passenger departed for Rochester, but Barton decided to make a pass over the lake, only about 10 feet above the ice. Unfortunately, the flag had disappeared during the night and Barton never saw the steel wire. His landing gear snagged it, and the Fairchild 24 flipped over on its back. Barton and his passenger sustained minor injuries, but the wooden propeller was smashed to bits and the wings and tail section were also badly damaged.

Jack Parker, who operated a garage on Genesee Street, brought the wreckage back to the Rochester Airport. During the next two months, the plane was completely rebuilt.

But in an oversight, no one remembered to check the crankshaft alignment. This problem made for a rough engine on full throttle but otherwise didn't affect the plane's ability to function. I was lucky enough to be invited by Pete to fly his plane. It was a joy.

About three years later, George Cheatham, who flew for Gannett Newspapers and later went on to become chief pilot for Braniff

Airlines, and Ralph Burford, who worked for Pete Barton (he later became a captain with American Airlines) took the plane for a little spin. I was sitting in the front cockpit of our Waco F2 with a student, waiting for the plane to land. It rolled to a stop, but then just sat there. "Come on, George, get the @#*& thing off the runway," I muttered.

But when both pilots climbed out and started pushing the plane off the runway, I saw what happened. Not only had they lost the propeller, but the crankshaft had gone along with it, having snapped off at the crankcase.

Fortunately, Cheatham had had enough altitude to glide to a safe landing. A few weeks later, when a new crankshaft and propeller were installed, the Warner engine ran as smoothly as a sewing machine.

Incidentally, in 1937, a young couple, determined to elope in a hurry, hired Robinson Air Service to fly them to Cleveland because New York State had a three-day waiting period for a marriage license, and they just couldn't wait.

Arriving at Cleveland about midnight, they were dismayed to learn that Ohio had enacted a law similar to New York's. So they decided to return to Rochester. The Stinson Reliant landed about 3:30 am on the northwest runway but didn't taxi in.

About 10 minutes later, the pilot came walking into the operations office, slightly embarrassed. His plane had run out of gas as he landed. If that had happened five minutes earlier, he would have had a forced landing in total darkness, with tragedy a virtual certainty.

It's not known if the couple ever married.

Stan Smith and His Glider

A few years ago, I had a chance encounter with the popular and highly regarded TV journalist Hugh Downs when we were catching flights out of Boston's Logan Airport.

Never passing up the opportunity to "talk shop" with other aviation buffs, I told him about an aeronautical engineer from Bell Aircraft in Niagara Falls named Stanley Smith.

Smith was an avid glider enthusiast who had achieved fame of sorts by winning a national glider championship in the 1930s. On a certain September morning in 1953, he took off in his glider on a cross-country flight as part of the National Glider Meet.

It so happened that this particular flight was worth remembering, and the story was circulated by some controllers at the Chemung County Airport in Elmira, New York, one of whom told it to me.

Smith had taken off from a place called Harris Hill in Elmira, and by the time "official" sunset had arrived, he was about to land at the old Idlewild Airport in New York, now known as Kennedy International. The glider was spotted by the watch supervisor, who advised his approach controller that "...that thing is moving too slowly to be a Piper Cub." When, to his surprise, he saw that it was actually a glider, he shouted, "It's heading for our field!" Fearing some sort of catastrophe, he notified all DC-3s, DC-6s, DC-4s, Corvair 247s, and Constellations to use extreme caution, and cleared the active runway so the small glider could land on the turf adjacent to the runway.

Furious, the watch supervisor ordered a pick-up truck to bring the pilot to the tower. When Smith was brought in, he got a severe tongue lashing for his "unmitigated gall" in landing at Idlewild, one of the busiest airports in the world.

But after the supervisor finished his tirade, Smith poked his finger at the supervisor's chest. "When was the last time you read the Civil Air Regulations, Buster?" The man instantly realized what Smith was driving at, because most controllers in those days were either licensed pilots themselves or had flown during World War II.

Smith then reminded the controller of the order of flight priorities at the time: first, fixed balloons; second, gliders; third, dirigibles; and fourth, powered aircraft (airplanes).

"Except for a goddamned balloon, I have priority over everything else you guys have operating out of this field," Smith reminded him.

Realizing that Smith was absolutely right, he could only offer Smith a sheepish apology.

Uncle Sam, though, had the last word. A few days later, a notice to airmen (NOTAM) was issued. It read: "All aircraft arriving at or departing from Idlewild Airport must be equipped with a functioning two-way radio." Gliders, of course, had no electric power for a standard two-way radio, and portable two-ways weren't invented until a few years later.

Sadly, Stan Smith is no longer with us. But I wouldn't doubt that his soul was carried to heaven in one of those cherished gliders.

Pilot Eleanor Roosevelt?

Among the staunchest women supporters for the advancement of aviation were pioneer aviator Amelia Earhart and First Lady Eleanor Roosevelt. Earhart was the first woman to cross the Atlantic and the first woman to fly it alone; Mrs. Roosevelt, a close friend of American Airlines president C.R. Smith, urged women through her newspaper column to use the airlines whenever possible.

It also appears that Mrs. Roosevelt was a budding aviatrix herself, as the following exchange of correspondence between these great women, discovered in the Franklin D. Roosevelt Library, reveals.

Aviatrix Jacqueline Cochran banded together a group of women pilots to form the Women's Auxiliary Service Pilots (WASP). And some of them could sting like their namesakes. There was the pilot who tried to get a WASP who was stretched out on a seat in the pilots' lounge to move over for some other weary flyers. She pulled no punches telling them all where to go!

THERE WERE BOUND TO BE SOME MISTAKES —

AMELIA EARHART

50 West 45th Street
New York City
November 20, 1933

My Dear Mrs. Roosevelt:

I just have received a clipping from Thursday's Star, with the story about your interest in flying. The article contains this line: "Amelia Earhart, and some of the First Lady's flying friends, have been circulating reports recently that Mrs. Roosevelt plans to learn to fly."

The wording troubles me a little. I hope you know that I do not "circulate reports." No one but Mr. Putnam and Dr. Smith knows through me of our conversations about the possibility of your learning to fly. Your examination certificate lies buried in my personal files.

If the time does come when you wish to take instruction, I shall be glad to help you in any way I can. In the meantime Gene Vidal seems to be urging the industry to new efforts by proposing quantity production of a little plane. Perhaps one will be ready for your first solo!

Sincerely yours,

Amelia Earhart

Mrs. Franklin D. Roosevelt,
The White House
Washington, D.C.

December 4, 1933

Dear Miss Earhart:

Of course that story was one of my fatal mistakes. I did not ask the young lady to see the copy, which is what I usually do. I did not say to her any more than I have said to the other girls many times now, that I would like to learn to fly, and that my husband convinced me that it was a waste of time to learn when I could not afford to buy a plane. She made it appear that my husband refused to buy me one — and of course I never would have asked him to do so.

The only thing I told her was that I passed the physical test. The rest of it was her own invention, and I was not the least troubled by "circulating reports" because I knew quite well nobody was giving it much thought.

If you ever come to Washington be sure to let me know. It was nice seeing you.

Very sincerely yours,

Eleanor Roosevelt

Miss Amelia Earhart
50 West 45th Street
New York, N.Y.

"This is London Calling" . . . 15 Years Later.

Photo by Lee D. Alderman

Paul Roxin and Edward R. Murrow Prepare for "Prospective on Peace" program. Paul's daughter, Wendy, gives the "woman's side view" of the preparations.

In 1960 Edward R. Murrow, famed TV news and interview person-appeared at the University of Rochester for the first "All-University Convocation."

By the second decade of the century, pilots and their aircraft were taking to the skies with such increasing frequency that "regulations" such as these — primitive by today's standards — were actually drawn up with the expectation that pilots would abide by them.

REGULATIONS FOR THE OPERATION OF AIRCRAFT
Commencing January 1920
Published by the U.S. Army War Office

1. Don't take the machine into the air unless you are satisfied it will fly.
2. Never leave the ground with the motor leaking.
3. Don't turn sharply when taxiing. Instead of turning sharp, have someone lift the tail around.
4. In taking off, look at the ground and the air.
5. Never get out of a machine with the motor running until the pilot relieving you can reach the engine controls.
6. Pilots should carry hankies in a handy position to wipe off goggles.
7. Riding on the steps, wings, or tail of a machine is prohibited.
8. In case the engine fails on takeoff, land straight ahead regardless of obstacles.
9. No machine must taxi faster than a man can walk.
10. Never run motor so that blast will blow on other machines.
11. Learn to gauge altitude, especially on landing.
12. If you see another machine near you, get out of the way.
13. No two cadets should ever ride together in the same machine.
14. Do not trust altitude instruments.
15. Before you begin a landing glide, see that no machines are under you.
16. Hedge-hopping will not be tolerated.
17. No spins on back or tail slides will be indulged in as they unnecessarily strain the machines.

18. If flying against the wind and you wish to fly with the wind, don't make a sharp turn near the ground. You may crash.
19. Motors have been known to stop during a long glide. If pilot wishes to use motor for landing, he should open throttle.
20. Don't attempt to force machine onto ground with more than flying speed. The result is bouncing and ricocheting.
21. Pilots will not wear spurs while flying.
22. Do not use aeronautical gasoline in cars or motorcycles.
23. You must not take off or land closer than 50 feet to the hanger.
24. Never take a machine into the air until you are familiar with its controls and instruments.
25. If an emergency occurs while flying, land as soon as possible.

During World War II there was never a dearth of instructions for pilots, crews and, in this case, new paratroopers learning to jump from aircraft in flight. This addendum is one of many "guidelines," most certainly apocryphal, dished out by the jumpmaster.

Addendum to Our Flight Plan

1. When you leap from the plane yell "Geronimo!" He was a brave and famous Indian warrior.
2. Pull the rip cord with your right hand.
3. If, for any reason, the chute fails to open, merely stick your thumbs under your armpits and flap your arms, and you will gracefully glide to a safe landing.

As one tale goes, after the last recruit had jumped from the plane, the jumpmaster closed the door on the C-47, sat in one of the bucket seats, and was about to light up a cigar when he heard a pounding on the side of the plane. He flung open the door to find one of his recruits wildly flapping his arms and yelling, "Sarge, what did you say the name of that Indian was?"

Mark Hare and his wife Kim.

The GPA: A Group That Tells No
How-I-Won-the-War Stories

By Mark Hare

Their stories are simple, understated and salted with humor, much of it at their own expense. They are living memorials of World War II, national treasures who will not be long with us — men *and* women from whom we can learn a great deal, men and women who celebrate Memorial Day as it was intended.

They call themselves the Geriatric Pilots Association, a name befitting an organization whose members know from their experiences of war how to keep life and themselves in perspective.

I met some of their members during one of their occasional visits to area high schools, where they tell their stories to students who listen with rapt attention.

Marshall "Mitch" Zinter flew 35 B-17 missions over Europe and is still trim enough to wear his flight suit. He brought along pictures of his crew — men he has kept in touch with for 50 years, and he also displayed a copy of the art printed on the nose of his bomber — a reproduction of a Varga girl he and his crew dubbed "Victory Virgin."

Air Force Lt. Richard Warboys, who few 78 missions in his P-47 Thunderbolt fighter, told the kids of his unique vantage point for the D-Day invasion.

"The troops on the beach at Normandy couldn't pick up the radio signals from England. So I flew up and down the English Channel at 32,000 feet, relaying the messages from the Allied command center to the invading forces.

"It was like being in a theater," he said, "and looking behind the curtain before it opened."

Lt. Col. Norman Levy, as a young Lieutenant, completed 31 missions at the age of 19. This picture was taken during an R&R session.

Norm Levy, a B-17 navigator, read song lyrics that captured the bittersweet sentiment of the fly boys.

"I wanted wings...until I got the goddamn things;
...If you'd thought a little faster,
you'd have joined the quartermaster,
buster."

That thought must have crossed Colin Storey's mind once or twice. On his first bombing mission over southeastern Germany, then-1st Lt. Storey's B-17 lost two engines and part of its tail to enemy fire. He made it back to England, but the plane became a "parts job" used to repair other bombers.

Storey described his 27th mission, when he fell out of formation. "Usually when that happens, you're duck soup," he recounted, "but the heavy cloud cover bought me a little time. I lost a couple of engines but was able to limp to Belgium for an emergency landing and avoid bailing out over Germany.

"We always knew when we were in for a tough mission," he explained "because we'd get fresh eggs for breakfast. Otherwise we got powdered eggs!"

Dawn Seymour was among the first WASPs (Women Air Service Pilots) and learned to fly B-17s and B-26s. She wasn't allowed to fly combat runs, but she did fly training missions — sometimes trailing targets our pilots and gunners used for practice. It didn't sound like a real safe job to me. But what Seymour treasures most are the friendships.

"Every time we have a reunion," she said, "everybody comes. We know there won't be many more of them."

Everything these pilots say is matter-of-fact. "Nobody in this group tells how-I-won-the-war stories," Paul Roxin told me. They know that victory came at a terrible price and that they were among the lucky ones.

"We were just ordinary people, just like you," Mitch Zinter told the kids. "We were young and weren't supermen, but they whipped us into pretty good pilots."

And they've been friends ever since. They won the total war that saved the world from total tyranny. But as you listen to them, you can tell that everything they did, they did for their friends — and they'd do it all again if called upon.

Tora! Tora! Tora! Hell No!
UCLA - UCLA - Hip-Hip-Hooray!

In early 1945, marine pilot Bob Ferris, now of Rochester, New York, was stationed in the South Pacific, on one of the Caroline Islands – a tiny strip just 3,200 feet long. The aircraft carrier *Essex* dropped anchor offshore to use the island's air strip to test new pilots.

Ferris remembers talking to crew members about a recent Kamikaze mission in which hundreds of Japanese pilots attacked U.S. ships. One pilot "did a water landing and bailed out and briefly displayed a sign reading UCLA." After the incident, small boats went out to look for survivors. The pilot was seen waving his arms and shouting "UCLA, UCLA." It turns out he was a Japanese-American who attended UCLA and had been visiting his grandparents in Japan when the war broke out. Eventually, the Japanese found out that he had a pilot's license and conscripted him into the air force. When he saw his chance to break away and survive, he knew the magic word: UCLA.

What Goes Around Comes Around
(But Should It Take 67 Years?????)

At the time of my graduation from high school in June of 1934, this remarkable nation of ours was starting to slowly emerge from the Great Depression. During that summer, a new vendor made his appearance at the Rochester Airport, none other than one of the founders of the Wegman's food chain. Unable to refrain from years of marketing, he became an agent for Havoline Aviation Motor Oil.

Each month, he would visit the airport, and sell a case of motor oil to the four flying services at the airport, all of whom had previously used Kendall Oil. Each case weighed approximately 40 pounds, too heavy for Mr. Wegman to lift, so I would deliver each case, and then after being thanked, would go about my regular duties.

Sixty-seven years later, in the summer of 2001, my wife, Bea, having seen a garden statue of a frog playing a cello (her instrument) at Wegmans, purchased the small garden figurine and decided that for my birthday, she would purchase the frog playing the clarinet which is my instrument. At the tail end of their season at their Pittsford, NY, store, the frog with the clarinet, was completely out of stock. There were other wind and brass instruments but no clarinet. With the help of a dedicated clerk, calls were made to other Wegmans stores, but to no avail. Finally, Bea found out the name of the importer of the Chinese-made sculpture, and after several days, she was notified that a clarinet had been located, and it would be shipped to the Pittsford store.

Two days before my birthday on September 23rd, Bea received a call from the store that the frog indeed had arrived, and when she went to pick it up, it was already gift-wrapped! When she inquired as to the price, she was told by the very generous store manager that because she had gone to so much trouble to locate the gift, she should accept it as a gift from Wegmans.

As we all sat down for dinner, with the gift on the table, I could barely contain myself. I was looking forward to seeing "my clarinet" (no longer a complete surprise!) because I was a member of the Irondequoit Concert Band and I envisioned taking it to rehearsal as a "show and tell" gag for the Conductor Russ Thomas.

Upon opening the package, 'lo and behold, we were shocked. In the box was not a clarinet at all, but a tuba!

All I could think of was saying to my wife, "Here you are a graduate of the Eastman School of Music (Class of '49), and you can't distinguish a tuba from a clarinet! For shame!"

To Danny Wegman, president of Wegman's, thank you; case closed!

Recalling "A Date Which Will Live In Infamy" at the Bagel Bin Cafe

Geriatric Pilot's Association, commemorating Pearl Harbor Day, December 7, 1941, at the Bagel Bin Cafe, Brighton, New York, December 7, 2002.

Lt. Marshall Zinter, B-17 Pilot, 8th Air Force, speaking with an interested spectator.

Geriatric Pilots Association

Geriatric Pilots Association
Membership Roster

Estey, Allan, Aetm 2c, USN Res.
Ettenson, Bernard, Col., USAAF
Fauth, Paul, 1st Lt., USAAF
Fergusson, David, 1st Lt., USAAF
Feeks, Thomas, Capt., USN
Ferris, Robert, Maj., USMC
Finger, Kenneth, 1st Lt., USAAF
Finkle, Jack, 1st Lt., USAAF
Fisher, Donald, Lt. Col., USAAF
Forsyth, Jack, Lt. USN
Garrison, Lloyd*
Gaston, Arthur, Col., USAAF
Geiser, Donald, Capt., USAAF
Gilman, John, Lt., USN Res.
Gleason, Huck, Flt. Off., USAAF
Golding, William, S. Sgt., USMC
Greer, George, Capt., USAAF
Haelen, John, 2d Lt., USAAF
Haidt, Forbes, Maj., USMC
Hanley, Edward, WWII History Buff
Hartman, Herbert, Col., USMC
Hawken, Charles, Maj., USMC
Hawkes, Hugh, 2d Lt., USAAF
Hazen, Phil, E4, USAAF
Heard, Warren, Lt. (Jg), USN Res.
Heier, Fredrick, 1st Lt., USAAF
Hoff, John, Capt., USN Res.
Hoff, Robert*
Hogle, Edward, Maj., USAAF
Holderbaum, Charles, ROTC
Hollingsworth, Jack. 1st. Lt., USAAF
Horton, Robert*
Houston, Claud, Cpt., USA
Hubbard, Raymond, Civilian Pilot,
            USAAC Inst.
Johnson, Robert, Capt., USMC
Jones, Hugh, S. Sgt., USA
Kadar, Bob*
Kenning, Charles, Lt. Col., USAAF

Allard, Albert, Maj. USAF
Allan, John, CU2 Army
Ash, Dick, Private Pilot
Bacon, Paul, Lt., USN Res.
Bailey, Dick, Maj., USAAF
Baker, Jim, 1st. Lt., USAAF
Begandy, Bob*
Bennett, Dick, Maj., USAAF
Bent, John, Lt. Col., USAAF
Bent, June., 2d Lt., WASP USAAF
Bowers, Alfred, Cpl., USAAF
Britt, Ed, 2d Lt., USA Sig. Corps
Bushong, Al, Lt. Col., USAAF
Caldwell, John, Capt., USAAF
Campbell, Bruce, Col., USA
Caplan, David, Civilian Pilot
Carroll, Ken, Capt., USMC Res.
Clark, Jonathon, Lt. Col., USAAF
Clemow, Joe, Capt., USAAF
Cole, Dave, Capt., USAAF Res.
Colfer, Joe, Lt., USN Res.
Coonan, Joe, Lt., USAAF
Cooper, Sam, Lt. Comdr, USN Res.
Crapsey, Art, 1st Lt., USAAF
Crawford, Dick, Capt., USAAF
Dake, Robert, 1st Lt., USAAF
Danlyshyn, Michael, Cpl., USAAF
Davis, Bob*
DePrez, Bob, Lt. USN
Dieck, Bill, 1st Lt., USAAF
Doe, Norman*
Doyle, John, 1st Lt., USA
Dublin, Bob, Lt., USN Res.
Dunn, George, Aviation Safety, FAA
Eckert, Arnie, 1st Lt., USA
Ehrlich, Harold, Lt. Col., USAAF
Engstrom, Harry, Pfc., USAAF

Kinyon, Charles, 1st Lt., USAAF
Kiseleski, Joseph, Lt., USAAF
Kittrel, John, Capt., USAAF
Klein, Jerard, Cpl., USMC
Knittle, William, Capt., USMC
Koss, George, 1st Lt., USAAF
Krozel, Walter, 1st. Lt., USAAF
Landsman, Richard, USAAF
Lasher, John, Cpl., Ordinance
Lengyel, Albert, M. Sgt., USAAF
Lennox, Thomas, Lt., USN Res.
Lapinski, Hank, Maj., USAAF
Levy, Norman, 1st Lt., USAAF
Luke, Lloyd, Flight Officer, RCAF
Magraw, Gil, Cpl., AACS
McCambridge, Robert, Lt., USN Res.
McCrae, Robert, PFC, Photo Recon.
McDill, Donald, Photm 2c, USN
McGinn, Fred, Capt. American Air.
Moffett, Janet, "Lady Bird"
Mosman, Bob, Maj., USAAF
Mueller, Richard, Capt., USAAF
Mulford, Fritz, Comdr., USN
Naber, Leo, Cpl., Quartermaster
Nemerow, David, Maj., USAAF
Newmark, Bernie, Maj., USAAF
Noon, Cyril, Capt, USAAF
Norman, Alfred, 1st Lt., USAAF
O'Connell, Thomas*
Paine, Robert, 2d Lt., USAAF
Pankratz, Elmer, Maj., USAAF
Parker, Robert, 2d Lt., USA
Ramsey, George, Lt. (Jg), USN
Rappl, Norbert, Maj. Gen., USA
Redfield, Alva, Lt. Comdr., USN Res.
Rice, William, Capt., USAAF
Rosenthal, Lauren, 1st Lt., USAAF
Roxin, Paul, CAA, Instructor USAAF
Santee, Don, Pfc., USA
Schantz, John*
Schmidt, Charlie. S. Sgt., USAAF
Schnabel, Albert, Lt., USAAF
Scott, Charles, M. Sgt., USAAF

Scott, William G.*
Seefried, John, Chief Builder
Seymour, Dawn, WASP
Smith, John, Civilian Flt. Instr.
Spiers, Paul, 1st Lt., USAAC
Stark, George, Lt. Comdr., USN Res.
Steinorth, Al, Lt., USN
Stevenson, Bob, 1st Lt.,USAAC
Storey, Colin, Lt. Col., USAAF
Suter, Martin,. Cmdr., USN Res.
Sweeting, Walter, Lt. (Jg), USN
Teachman, Stanley, Chummey Proj.
Terhune, Jim, 1st Lt., USAAF
Thieme, Art, USN
Tripp, George, Lt. Col., USAAF
Trudeau, Edward, Capt., USAAF
Tucker, Robert, Lt. Col., USAAF
Turner, Dwight, Maj., USAAF
Valley, Russell*
Vangellow, Paul, Cpl., USMC
Wadeikis, Walter, Lt., USN
Walden, William, USN
Warboys, Richard, 1st Lt., USAAF
Ward, Ralph, Flt. Eng., USAAF
Webber, Wayne, Flt. Off., USAAF
Weidner, Carl, Capt., USAF
Wetmore, Robert, Cpl., USMC
Wesley, Lee, Capt., USAAF
Wilkins, Edwin, Capt., USAAF
Williams, Jack, Lt. (Jg), USN
Williams, Kenneth, Lt. Col., USAAF
Williams, Warren, 1st Lt., USAAF
Willis, James, Gm 3c, USN
Wilmot, Gerald, Civ. Mil. Pil. Inst.
Wise, John, Comdr, USNR
Witmer, Charles, 1st Lt., USAAF
Wright, Claude, Civ. Inst., USAAF Res.
Yackiw, Charles, 2d Lt., USAAF
Zinter, Marshall. 1st Lt., USAAF

*Service data not available as of publication date

204

Addendum
Geriatric Pilots Association
Current List of New Members

Name	Rank	Group
Barker, Jack	ET3	USN
Bishop, Robert	T/Sgt	US Army
Brice, Bill		Private Pilot
Brigenbaugh, J. Ross	Lt. Col	USAAF
Brockman, Roy	1st Lt.	USAAF
Brown, Morrie		Civilian Pilot
Burger, Fred	1st Lt.	USAAF
Chlebowski, Ed	T/Sgt.	USAAF
Cone, Edward	CPL	USAAF
Conolly, Bill		Aviation Buff
Cox, Ted		Civilian Pilot
Culbertson, Norm	Lt. Col	USAAF
Delles, Charles		
DelMonte, Steven		
DeMallie, Howard	1st Lt.	USAAF
Eltscher, Louis		Aviation Buff
Esmay, Edward	2nd Lt.	US Army
Felstead, Ron		Commercial Pilot
Fitzgerald, Robert	Flt. Engr.	UAL
Fribance, John		Civilian Pilot
Frisina, Robert	2nd Lt.	USAAF
Halik, Frederick		Commercial Pilot
Hall, George		
Hanna, Michael	Capt.	AAL
Hayes, Ralph	Col.	USAAF
Hoefler, Patricia		Private Pilot
Holtz, Barry		Civilian Pilot
Hughes, Richard		Aviation Buff
Hughes, Don	2nd Lt.	USAAF
Ireland, Corydon		Aviation Buff
Kauffman, Lee		Civilian Pilot
Kennedy, Spence		USN
Kinyon, Charles	1st Lt.	USAAF
Kitt, Ross	Capt.	US Army
Lee, William	Lt.	USAAF
Lockemeyer, Bob		Aviation Buff
Mack, Walter		Civilian Pilot
Martin, Walt		Commercial Pilot
McGarry, Bill	1st Lt.	USAAF

Name	Rank	Group
Malchoff, Doc		Civilian Pilot
McCaughey, Roger		
Maxwell, Tom		Aviation Buff
Mincer, Robert		Civilian Pilot
Moran, Harry		Commercial Pilot
Nesbitt, Peter	Lt. (Jg)	USN
Notebaert, Richard	Capt.	USAAF
Osadnick, Jerome	Capt.	USAAF
Paddock, Dave		
Park, Richard	Lt.	USN
Pickins, James	T/Sgt.	USAAF
Piendel, Ray	T/Sgt.	USAAF
Province, Jack	2nd Lt.	USAAF
Purdy, Walter	Lt. Col.	USAAF
Redmond, Eugene		Commercial Pilot
Reed, Art	Lt. (Jg)	USN
Roberts, Ed		Civilian Pilot
Roth, Charles	1st Lt.	USAAF
Schwarz, Peter		Private Pilot
Seymour, Ed		Glider Pilot
Shaw, Bill		Commercial Pilot
Slocomb, Robert		Commercial Pilot
Smart, Jerry	Flt. Eng.	USAAF
Smith, Clark		Aviation Buff
Soule, Gardner		Corporate Pilot
Sovocool, William	Maj.	USAAF
Spalty, Irv	Ens.	USN
Starks, Myron	Lt. Col.	USAAF
Stephens, Clyde	Lt.	USN
Stevenson, John		
Ten Haken, Dick		Private Pilot
Treat, Charles		USN Aviation
Trimble, Arthur	1st Lt.	USAAF
Vanderhoof, Jon.	Capt.	USAAF
Van Houten, Gene	1st Lt.	USAAF
Warner, Gena	1st Lt.	USAAF
Weckesser, Joe		
Wellers, Chuck	1st Lt.	USAAF
Willis John		
Wise, William		Aviation Buff
Zavada, Roland	Capt.	USAAF

Index

ISBN 141200297-4